BRANCH LINES AROUND PRESTON AND LANCASTER

Featuring Fishergate Hill (Goods),
Preston Dock including the Ribble Steam Railway,
Longridge, Whittingham Hospital, Knott End, Lancaster Old Goods Line,
Glasson Dock, St. George's Quay and Lancaster Power Station Branches

Roy Davies

Front cover: Ex-LMS class 5 4-6-0 no. 45019 allocated to Springs Branch depot, Wigan, finds itself on humble duties between Pilling and Garstang Town as it returns an empty coal wagon from Pilling to Preston on midsummer day 21st June 1961. The train is slowing for the crossing at Cogie Hill where the train crew will be responsible for opening and closing the gates before proceeding to Garstang Town prior to its rejoining the main line at Garstang and Catterall station. No. 45019 was the last locomotive of the first order for the construction of 20 such engines built at Crewe Works in 1935 and was not withdrawn until May 1967. (Noel Machell)

Back cover picture: Manning Wardle 0-6-0T Knott End *believed to be taken by the loco facilities at Knott End station. This locomotive was bought new in 1908 for the opening of the extension of the railway from Pilling to Knott End. Although the extension was built by the new company known as the Knott End Railway the locomotive carries the old initials G&KER on its side tanks. It stayed on the railway until the grouping but was almost immediately withdrawn and scrapped by the LMS in 1923. (Knott End Collection)*

Back cover map: Railway Clearing House map (edited), dated 1947. The routes of the album are shown with dotted lines.

ACKNOWLEDGEMENTS

I am very grateful for the assistance received from many of those mentioned in the credits, also from Mark Bartlett, Godfrey Croughton, Rob Daniels, Jackie Dove, Geoff Gartside, Henry Henson, Chris Howard, Norman Langridge, Mike Norris, Brian Read, David and Dr Susan Salter, Paul Shannon, Michael Stewart and Andy Stoddon. Special thanks also to local author, Dave Richardson.

Published March 2024

ISBN 978 1 910356 82 1

© Middleton Press Ltd, 2024

*Cover design and
  Photographic enhancement
  Deborah Esher
Production Cassandra Morgan*

*Published by
  Middleton Press Ltd
  Camelsdale Road
  Haslemere
  Surrey
  GU27 3RJ*
Tel: 01730 813169
*Email: info@middletonpress.co.uk
www.middletonpress.co.uk*

Railway company abbreviations:
English, Welsh & Scottish Railway (EWS)
Garstang & Knott End Railway (G&KER)
Knott End Railway (KER)
Lancaster & Carlisle Railway (L&CR)
Lancaster & Preston Junction Railway (L&PJR)
Lancashire & Yorkshire Railway (L&Y)
London Midland & Scottish Railway (LMS)
London & North Western Railway (LNWR)
North Union Railway (NUR)
Preston & Longridge Railway (P&LR)
Fleetwood Preston & West Riding Junction Railway (FP&WRJR)
Preston & Wyre Railway (P&WR)
Ribble Steam Railway (RSR)
West Coast Main Line (WCML)
West Lancashire Railway (WLR)

Printed and bound by CPI Group (UK) Ltd, Croydon, CR0 4YY

SECTIONS

1. Fishergate Hill (Goods)   1- 2
2. Preston Dock (Ribble) Branch (Victoria Quay)   3-33
3. Preston & Longridge Railway   34-60
4. Whittingham Hospital Railway   61-64
5. Garstang & Knott End Railway   65- 88
6. Lancaster Old Goods Line   89- 93
7. Glasson Dock Branch   94-105
8. St. George's Quay Branch   106-113
9. Lancaster Power Station Branch   114-120

CONTENTS

95 Ashton Hall Halt	98 Glasson Dock	34 Maudland
75 Cogie Hill Halt	55 Grimsargh	73 Nateby
96 Conder Green	61 Grimsargh Hospital Halt	76 Pilling
39 Deepdale	83 Knott End	80 Preesall
47 Deepdale Street	94 Lancaster	51 Ribbleton
65 Garstang & Catterall	57 Longridge	64 Whittingham Hospital
67 Garstang Town		

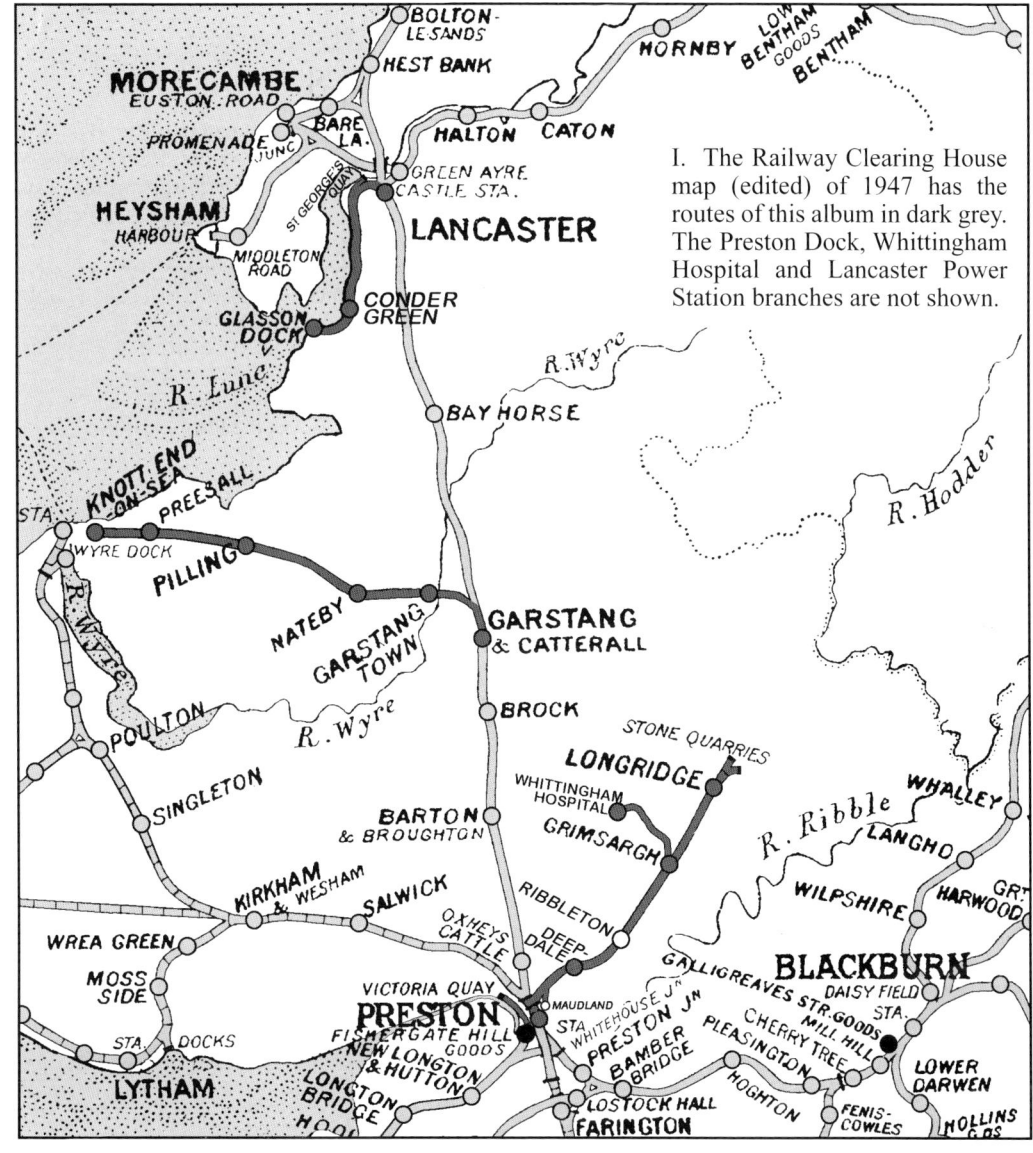

I. The Railway Clearing House map (edited) of 1947 has the routes of this album in dark grey. The Preston Dock, Whittingham Hospital and Lancaster Power Station branches are not shown.

GEOGRAPHICAL SETTING

The lines covered in this album ran just above sea level with the exception of the Lancaster Old Goods Line and the Longridge branch that climbed steadily throughout as it headed towards Longridge Fell; the most southerly hill in England that has the word 'fell' in its name. With freight services continuing on the Longridge branch until 1967 a crossing was needed to take the line over the Preston bypass that later became a section of the M6. With closure of the line and widening of the M6 a replacement bridge was constructed that now carries a footpath across the motorway. Other features on the branch include a 50ft (15.2m) tunnel just beyond Longridge.

The Fishergate Hill Branch remained on a level with the former West Lancashire Railway River Ribble crossing. The Knott End Railway crossed the River Wyre, Pilling Water and the Lancaster Canal and the only significant structures were a road bridge built over the line, rather than the usual level crossing, and another bridge built in the 1920s taking the Garstang by-pass over the line.

After climbing out of Lancaster on the 1 in 98 to Lancaster Old Junction the goods line remained on the level with no geological features of note. With Preston station approximately 89ft (27m) above sea level, the Ribble branch to the dock had a descent of 1 in 29 and through a 145yd (132.6m) tunnel before reaching the exchange sidings. The Glasson Dock and St. George's Quay branches shared the 1 in 50 descent from Lancaster station, which was around 75ft (23m) above sea level, while the Power Station line had a 1 in 78 descent that carried it over the Water Street crossing.

All maps are derived from 25ins to 1 mile editions dated 1912-13, with north at the top, unless otherwise indicated.

HISTORICAL BACKGROUND

Apart from the rump of the former Preston Dock railway network that serves the Total bitumen terminal and Ribble Steam Railway and Museum, all the branch lines covered in this album were closed and lifted long ago. There are traces of the Longridge branch at Maudland through the abandoned Miley Tunnel and part of the route from Blackpool Road is now a cycle/footpath. There are also occasional traces of the former branch to Knott End in open fields while much of the Glasson Dock branch has been converted into a cycle way and the bridge that carried the Power Station branch over Water Street in Lancaster is still in place.

Fishergate Hill (Goods)

Following acquisition of the West Lancashire Railway (WLR) by the Lancashire & Yorkshire Railway (L&YR) in 1897, it was not long after in 1900 that passenger services on the line were diverted to Preston's East Lancs platforms after which the terminus and yard became a freight facility and the line a secondary route. Apart from freight operations, rail tours ran from there during Preston Guild festivals and empty excursion coaching stock was stabled at the end of the branch on such occasions. By 1968 all track had been lifted in the goods yard and station area and the bridge taking the former WLR over the Ribble was part-demolished and now carries a gas main across the river. Following closure of the line, the station building survived and was used by a commercial undertaking until 1976 after which the site was developed for housing.

Preston Dock (Ribble) Branch

In 1846, in conjunction with the Ribble Navigation Company, the North Union Railway (NUR) obtained powers to build a branch just south of Preston station to Victoria Quay on the north bank of the River Ribble to carry coal from the Wigan area to the river for onward shipment. In 1884 construction of the port began with the diversion of the River Ribble and excavation of the new basin. In July 1885 the dock's foundation stone was laid by Queen Victoria's eldest son, Albert Edward the Prince of Wales, after whom the basin was named. The port was officially opened on 25th June 1892.

Throughout its history the dock handled a wide variety of cargoes. Incoming goods would include raw cotton, timber, china clay, fruit (primarily from the West Indies), wheat, horses, cattle, coal, petroleum products, fishmeal, fertilisers and raw materials for paper making. Outgoing vessels were mostly loaded with cotton and other textiles from local mills together with goods manufactured in and around Preston.

Apart from the cranes, grain silos, oil tanks and other paraphernalia associated with a port, the rail-served Dick, Kerr & Co works, later subsumed into the English Electric group, was located on a large site in the northeast corner of the dock.

In the 1920s, the rail line from the original branch was extended along both sides of the dock and a network of lines developed as the docks grew with 27 miles (43km) of standard gauge track at its peak leading to an increase in the volume of goods handled by the port.

The period 1960 to 1972 was the busiest in the dock's history but, thereafter, the port experienced a reduction in trade and a noticeable fall in revenue due to containerised cargo and larger ships that could not navigate the shallow River Ribble despite continued dredging. This effectively signalled closure of the port and, in 1981, an Act of Parliament was passed to close the docks with the last official day of operation being 31st October of that year.

The railway remained in operation after closure of the docks with up to nine trains per week delivering gasoline to the Petrofina storage tanks on Chain Caul Way, located in what is now the Anchorage Business Park; the company ceased operations in 1992 and the gasoline facility was demolished. This left just one company, Lancashire Tar Distillers, also located in the business park, that operated three weekly trains delivering crude bitumen from the Lindsey Oil Refinery in Lincolnshire to the distilling plant. At that time the bitumen terminals at Ashton-in-Makerfield and Preston Dock were served by a combined train. The Preston Dock service finished in 1995 and the company switched to road transport due to damage to an overbridge on the branch and, as a consequence, trains ran only to the Ashton-in-Makerfield terminal that later closed in 2003.

In 2001, a Freight Facilities Grant of nearly £2 million was awarded to re-open the Preston Dock branch; it was a long process and, in December 2004, English, Welsh & Scottish Railway (EWS) finally ran the first revenue-earning service, by which time the plant had been sold to Total Fina Elf. EWS was acquired by Deutsche Bahn in June 2007 and in January 2015 Colas Rail took over haulage of the Preston Dock bitumen traffic.

With closure of the docks looming in 1980, plans were made to redevelop 380 acres (150 hectares) of the site for mixed use. 'Riversway', as it became known, includes extensive residential development, retail and leisure facilities and the basin features a public marina; all this led to removal of most of the rail infrastructure. In 1985 a single line was built across the new Preston Dock 1,000 tonne swing bridge and rejoined the existing line from the level crossing on Strand Road to serve the Total bitumen terminal along with the Ribble Steam Railway and Museum, which were all located at the western end of the Anchorage Business Park.

The Ribble Steam Railway started life as long ago as 1973, when a preservation centre was opened in the former L&YR shed at Derby Road (27C), Southport. Maintaining the shed was becoming too costly so a relocation plan was started and Preston Dock was chosen as the new location for the museum. The Southport Railway Museum closed finally in 1999. The project's new site now could be re-developed with workshops, platforms and a museum. The first building opened by the Ribble Steam Railway (RSR) was the workshop in 2001. Later the visitor centre was constructed, which contains the extensive museum, cafe, shop and platform.

In 2013, the Furness Railway Trust vacated its facilities at the Lakeside and Haverthwaite Railway and relocated to the Preston site where new accommodation has been built, which is shared with the RSR, and is used to house, restore and maintain the Trust's locomotives and other vehicles.

Preston & Longridge Railway

The Longridge branch built by the Preston & Longridge Railway (P&LR) started life on 1st May 1840 as a 6½ mile (10.4km) single-track tramway that ran from the Tootle Heights quarry to a terminus and yard at Deepdale Street, which was not connected to the national network. While its primary purpose was to haul ashlar sandstone to Preston there were basic passenger facilities at Longridge, Grimsargh and Deepdale Street. Wagons ran by gravity and/or were horse-drawn as necessary.

In 1846 the Fleetwood, Preston & West Riding Junction Railway (FP&WRJR) was formed with challenging plans to link Fleetwood with Leeds and Bradford. It was proposed to link the Preston & Wyre Railway (P&WR) with the P&LR in Preston and construct a new line from Grimsargh via Ribchester, Hurst Green and Clitheroe to Skipton, where it would join the proposed Leeds and Bradford Extension Railway (later the Midland Railway). In anticipation of the scheme going ahead the P&LR was leased to the FP&WRJR.

The P&WR terminus at Maudland was reached by crossing the then Lancaster & Preston Junction Railway mainline on the flat. In 1848 the P&LR was adapted for steam working and the FP&WRJR constructed a 1½ mile (2.4km) double-track extension from the P&WR at Maudland to what became Deepdale Junction passing through the 862 yard (788m) Miley Tunnel. This section was completed

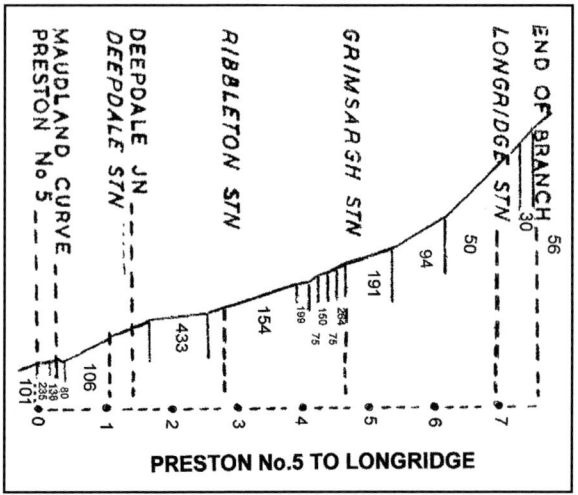

PRESTON No.5 TO LONGRIDGE

on 14th January 1850 but was the only work completed by the FP&WRJR as construction on the proposed extension from Grimsargh towards Clitheroe was soon abandoned along with earthworks and cuttings at Hurst Green that can still be seen today. In 1852, the FP&WRJR collapsed but the P&LR continued to operate the line and acquired the locomotives and rolling stock from the company in lieu of unpaid rent on the lease of its line.

In 1856, a revived FP&WRJR purchased the line and immediately commenced passenger services throughout starting with a new station at Maudland Bridge and another through Miley Tunnel at Deepdale Bridge. The original Deepdale Street terminus was closed to passengers but continued to be used for goods and later a coal concentration depot.

Ten years later, in 1866, plans to reach Yorkshire were again revived but, alarmed by the possibility of the Midland Railway acquiring the line in order to gain access to Preston, the LNWR and the L&YR purchased the FP&WRJR; the price to be paid for joint ownership was £8 per share (nominal value £12) and plans for the extension were shelved.

In 1885, the track layout at Maudland was altered to allow Longridge trains to run into Preston station on the LNWR line as did trains from Blackpool and Fleetwood. In the same year the demolished Maudland station was replaced by a goods station that continued to be used until 1990. The site is now occupied by the University of Central Lancashire student accommodation.

There was another plan to extend the railway in 1918 from Longridge to Yorkshire along the Loud and Hodder valleys to Whitewell, Tosside, Wigglesworth and on to Hellifield but the plan was never implemented. The plan was revived once again in connection with the Stocks Reservoir scheme in the Forest of Bowland supported by a Light Railway Order confirmed on 19th March 1924 but that also came to nothing.

In 2010, light rail manufacturer Trampower UK opened negotiations with Preston City Council and Lancashire County Council to use a segment of the former route as a tram demonstrator line. Initially, Trampower UK would use a few hundred yards of the line between Deepdale Street and the West View Leisure Centre with long-term ambitions to provide a service on the line from Junction 31A on the M6 to Preston station to be known as the Guild Line. The scheme was planned for opening in 2019. Perhaps the permanent red signal light at the start of the former branch says it all.

The first station after traversing the Miley tunnel opened by the FP&WRJR was Deepdale Bridge, a through station as a replacement for Deepdale Street the former terminus of the P&LR. The next station was Gamull Lane later named Ribbleton; there was also a short-lived station called Ribbleton that was opened towards Preston.

A little further to the east of what was to become the Preston bypass, later part of the M6 motorway, was a siding that led to the Red Scar Courtaulds textile factory. The site had its own power station that was coal-fired with fuel delivered by rail. With closure of the Red Scar factory in 1980 the line was cut back far enough to allow trains to reverse and be shunted to/from Deepdale Street.

The penultimate station was Grimsargh, which opened in 1840 and was rebuilt by the LNWR/L&YR in 1870; later a second Grimsargh station was opened to serve the Whittingham Hospital Railway. The final station to be opened on the route in 1840 was at Longridge.

Last but not least was the final section of the line to the Tootle Heights quarry. The Longridge ashlar sandstone quarried there was widely used in the construction in the region, for example: Lancaster and Bolton Town Halls; Preston Railway Station; Liverpool Docks and the Fishergate Baptist Church in Preston. In the 1970s a motor racing circuit was constructed in the former quarry. The roads used for the extremely short circuit at 0.43 miles (0.69km) were already in place when racing started in 1973; prior to that sprint events had been held at the former quarry. The site was sold in 1978 amid much rancour and is now a caravan park.

Until 1986, coal was delivered to Deepdale using the Speedlink network via Warrington Arpley yard. BR established its Speedlink Coal network and Deepdale was served by trains direct from Healey Mills via the Copy Pit line and amended in 1990 to run from Washwood Heath. In 1993, BR abandoned the household coal network, by then named Network Coal, although Deepdale was one of two household coal depots on the network to survive. It received occasional trainloads of coal from Gwaun-cae-Gurwen, Onllwyn or Coedbach collieries, as required. The last train to Deepdale ran in 1994 after which the branch was abandoned.

Whittingham Hospital Branch

The Whittingham Psychiatric Hospital was opened in 1873 and became the largest mental hospital in the United Kingdom. The hospital had a 2 mile (3.2km) private railway that ran from Grimsargh and transported coal, other goods and provided free transport for staff, patients and visitors alike. The railway was a private line operated by Lancashire County Council, opened in 1889. The line's first locomotive was scrapped in 1946 and a second engine was acquired in 1947 from the Southern Railway. This was a William Stroudley D1 class 0-4-2T tank engine and was named *James Fryers* in honour of the Chairman of the Hospital Management Committee. Serious boiler defects in 1956 curtailed the Stroudley's working career and it was scrapped later that year. It was the last serving member of that class. As a replacement Sentinel 100hp (75kW) shunter *Gradwell* was acquired from Bolton gas works but lasted only for 18 months before the line was closed on 30th June 1957.

Garstang & Knott End Railway

Referred to as the Garstang & Knot End Railway in the Act of Parliament of 1864, the 11½ mile (18.4km) G&KER was to run from Garstang & Catterall station on the Lancaster & Preston Junction Railway (L&PJR) mainline and on through Pilling to Knott End situated on the eastern side of the River Wyre estuary opposite Fleetwood. For most of the 19th century it was a single 't' in Knot End.

The railway was the brainchild of a group of local landowners, headed by Wilson F. France, the Squire of Rawcliffe. They believed strongly that a railway was essential in providing an outlet for the agricultural products to the likes of Preston and beyond. In the 1863 prospectus for the G&KER somewhat exaggerated claims were made such as an east/west route linking Knott End with Humberside and Tyneside and a harbour at Knott End to match or even surpass that at Fleetwood. The London and North Western Railway (LNWR) that was the owner/operator of adjacent lines was opposed to the proposed schemes and the prospectus was toned down accordingly.

From the outset the G&KER was beset with financial problems; for example, it could not raise subscriptions for the authorised share capital of £60,000 and, as a consequence, plans to go beyond Pilling were abandoned. Parliamentary approval for an extension in time to complete construction was given and in 1869 further authorisation was passed to increase the share capital to £100,000. The first locomotive the G&KER acquired was *Hebe,* along with rolling stock acquired by a group of debenture holders and, on 5th December 1870, the line from Garstang & Catterall to Pilling was opened with intermediate stations at Garstang Town and Nateby.

Initially the G&KER ran nine trains a day between Garstang & Catterall and Garstang Town of which two, sometimes three, would carry on to Pilling; from 1875 all trains ran to/from Pilling.

All services were mixed passenger and freight, and passengers could board/depart the train anywhere along the route by request. With lack of motive power, the G&KER introduced a novel idea for dealing with freight traffic; on the outward journey, wagons would be dropped off along the line as required and on return propelled back to their respective destinations.

The G&KER always seemed to lack funds and other resources; so much so, without a locomotive, passenger services were suspended on 11th March 1872 and a reduced horse-drawn freight service continued for a further two weeks. Thereafter the line was practically dormant, although it is understood that farmers anxious to get produce to market reverted to horse-drawn wagons, as necessary. In 1874 the debenture holders came to the rescue of the G&KER once again, when they acquired another locomotive, Manning Wardle 0-4-0ST *Union*. Freight services began again on 23rd February 1875 with a resumption of passenger services on 17th May 1875.

The G&KER continued to suffer financially and in 1878 it was placed in receivership. However in the succeeding 16 years its financial condition improved to the extent that it generated sufficient income to clear arrears for rolling stock rental and all debts reduced to £44,000 by 1898. On 12th August 1898 an Act was passed for the Knott End Railway (KER), formed by a group of investors, to extend the line from Pilling to the coast, although it was not until 1908 that the 4½ mile (7.2km) extension was completed. On 1st July of that year the KER acquired the G&KER and the line opened to passengers throughout on 1st August 1908. The cost of the acquisition and completion of the line was £180,000.

With the 11½ mile (18.4km) line fully operational to Knott End, it prospered from the carriage of freight; moss litter from around Knott End and Cogie Hill and salt from the United Alkali Company mining operations at Preesall together with coal deliveries to the factory. Two trains ran every day from the works to the KER line and by 1918 over 30,000 tons of salt left the works by rail and almost 8,000 tons of fuel and materials were brought in. Occasional use of the line in the summer months from 1906 to 1909 was made by artillery volunteers who brought their guns and horses to practice on Pilling sands.

All in all the KER was buoyant with both freight and passenger traffic at high levels culminating in the busiest period for the railway from around 1913. During World War I the salt traffic flourished due to the dislocation of shipping due to enemy action and the moss litter traffic also fared well due to the demand for horse bedding from the Army.

The Railways Act 1921 saw the establishment of the London Midland & Scottish Railway (LMS) that absorbed the KER and debenture holders associated with the line were rewarded by receiving equivalent LMS paper. While the LMS saw a decline in freight traffic, passenger services fared no better during the 1920s due mainly to the rapid growth and competition from road transport leading to passenger services being withdrawn throughout on 31st March 1930. Freight traffic persisted but the decline continued; so all that remained at Preesall was the mine and pumping station, which were closed in 1930 due to subsidence and other technical difficulties. Thereafter, the line was closed in stages; first the section from Knott End to Pilling on 13th November 1950; then Pilling to Garstang Town on 31st July 1963 and finally between the latter and Garstang & Catterall on 16th August 1965.

Both the G&KER and KER acquired their own locomotives from the outset; all were named and generally deemed suitable for the jobs in hand. Other than those pictured in this album, the following locomotives were acquired: 1870 Black Hawthorn 0-4-2ST *Hebe*; 1875 Hudswell Clark 0-6-0ST *Farmer's Friend* and 1885 Hudswell Clarke 0-6-0ST *Hope*.

In 1920, the KER hired an LNWR railmotor that carried out almost all of the passenger duties until cessation of the service in 1930. Very early on after the Grouping, the LMS drafted in a couple of ex-L&YR 0-6-2 tanks to cover goods traffic.

In 1903 the G&KER acquired some coaches from the Mersey Railway that were being auctioned when the Liverpool line was electrified and, when the line was extended to Knott End in 1908, the KER purchased eight bogie carriages from the Birmingham Carriage & Wagon Co., Smethwick, in anticipation of an increase in passenger traffic and a marked increase in comfort compared with the former six-wheeled sets used on the branch. These coaches were a big success until the early 1920s when competition from buses hit hard and the introduction of the LNWR railmotor more or less made them redundant. As freight traffic on the KER grew it procured a number of wagons of varying capacity to meet requirements peaking at the start of WWI. Salt appears to have been carried in wagons belonging to United Alkali.

By the slipway at Knott End, a sculpture commemorates painter L.S. Lowry's frequent visits to the village in the 1940s and 50s - sadly too late to have travelled there by train and alas there is no painting celebrating the railway.

Lancaster Old Line

The Lancaster & Preston Junction Railway line to its terminus at Penny Street was not a branch when it opened but the original main line from Preston to Lancaster. However it soon became a secondary line/siding once the L&PJR connected with the Lancaster & Carlisle Railway at Lancaster Old Junction and all passenger services transferred to Lancaster Castle station in 1849. The branch was referred to as 'Lancaster Old Line' by the control staff based in Preston. It boasted a goods shed and a small locomotive shed, known as Ripley Shed, a turntable and coal sidings etc. The line was truncated just short of the former passenger station that now houses NHS offices and was formerly a nurses hostel. Otherwise today little remains of the branch other than a remnant of the platform in the former goods yard that can be seen in the Royal Lancaster Infirmary car park off Ashton Road. Apart from trips to the coal and goods yard, southbound Saturday freight services were occasionally stabled in the branch due to the large number of passenger trains running south of Preston on a summer Saturday.

Glasson Dock Branch

As ships grew larger they experienced difficulty in navigating the River Lune as far as Lancaster and so the Port Commissioners decided to construct a dock at Glasson at the mouth of the river. It opened in March 1787 and could accommodate up to 25 vessels at that time. With the Lancaster Canal nearby, it was decided to open a connection to the port from Galgate and in 1825 the 2½ mile (4km) waterway was completed.

By 1830 over 10,000 tons of cargo passed through the port with the majority being transferred to the canal but it was nearly 60 years before the railway came to Glasson, although there were a number of abortive attempts to link the port with the national network. First to try was the P&WR and later the York & Lancaster Railway and, most notably, the Lancaster & Carlisle Railway (L&CR) in 1848. With the ongoing spat between the L&PJR and the L&CR, the latter announced it was planning to construct a line to Preston via Nateby with a branch to Glasson Dock; however, the disagreements evaporated when the L&CR acquired the L&PJR. The P&WR tried again and failed and the Midland Railway showed an interest in extending the line from Lancaster Green Ayre towards Glasson but that also came to nothing because the Port Commissioners backed the LNWR's plans developed in 1871. Plans that did not materialise for some time led to trade at Glasson Dock declining compared with Preston, Fleetwood and Morecambe that were all rail-served. Finally in 1883, after lengthy delays due to financial shortcomings, the LNWR completed the 5 mile (8km) line from Lancaster Castle to Glasson Dock together with a spur from Lancaster Marsh to St George's Quay. Freight traffic began in April 1883 and the railway carried iron ore, timber, wood pulp, cork and general cargo and coal in the other direction, while the first fare-paying passengers were carried a few months later on 9th July. There were two intermediate stations at Conder Green and the private request stop, Ashton Hall Halt. As well as the station at Glasson, there was a storage shed and station master's house. There was a line along the north side of the canal and dock basins and another down the riverside wharf known as the New Quay. Other than the fairly steep gradient of 1 in 50 up to Lancaster Castle station, the rest of the line was across low-lying land that was prone to occasional flooding.

While passenger traffic remained fairly consistent, there was no significant increase in freight workings despite the rail link; that is until 1898 when much larger quantities of iron ore were being imported from Spain for the Carnforth iron works. By 1905 trade at the docks started to decline once more when Heysham Harbour became fully operational and from which it never really recovered apart from extra freight carried during the two World Wars. Post-WWII freight never reached pre-war levels and the daily freight service then ran as required. Passenger services fared even worse due almost entirely to competition from the local bus service with the last train service leaving Glasson Dock on 6th July 1930. With nationalisation of the railways in 1948, BR (LMR) made its first attempt to close the branch but there was strong opposition from the Port Commissioners. Thereafter traffic was sporadic and so the section of the line from Freeman's Wood to Glasson Dock was closed in September 1964. This afforded a head shunt and access to the St. George's Quay sidings. With all track lifted much of the former branch to Glasson Dock is now a popular cycleway that starts at the Lune Millennium Bridge in Lancaster.

St. George's Quay Branch

Completed in 1883 the Quay branch was reached by a spur off the Glasson Dock line at Lancaster Marsh. The freight to and from the quay was not related to Glasson Dock activities to the extent that the two lines descending from Lancaster Castle were operated mainly as two bi-directional lines serving Glasson Dock on the left and the Quay Goods line to the right. With the Glasson Dock branch truncated a little way beyond Lune Mills in 1964 the St George's Quay branch survived a few more years. The branch served the District Engineer's depot and workshop, various Williamson's factories and mills, some shipping and the city's gas works. Later on, the branch was utilised in connection with the reconstruction of the Carlisle Bridge that took the West Coast Mainline over the River Lune. The branch along the quay was closed on 30th June 1969 leaving only a stub serving the Engineer's depot and Williamson's power station until final closure on 4th April 1971.

Lancaster Power Station Branch

With final closure of the former Midland main line from Morecambe and Heysham on 3rd June 1967, Lancaster Power Station had to be kept supplied with coal and a branch from Lancaster Castle station was created. The single spur from Lancaster Castle station to Green Ayre, de-energised in

1966, formed the first part of the branch to the power station complex. As the lines through the former Midland station and beyond were taken out of use and lifted, a single line was laid through to the power station and in part at a higher grade, notably when crossing the Greyhound Bridge that had been converted for road traffic carrying the northbound A6 and westbound A589 over the River Lune. Since 1967 the line was classed as an 'up/down siding' so was not under signalling control. However, from 1972, with the opening of the level crossing over the road, the line between Lancaster No. 4 signal box and the Power Station was worked in accordance with the One Train Working Regulations and the train staff, when not on use, was kept at Lancaster Station. After the 1973 re-signalling that rule was amended slightly. The line was lifted in April 1976 so presumably the power station had sufficient coal to continue operating until closure on 26th October of that year.

PASSENGER SERVICES

With the transfer of West Lancs passenger services from Fishergate Hill to Preston's East Lancs platforms, it was a case of passengers no more on the freight line save for occasional excursions and rail tours. The Preston Dock branch was always freight only but the Ribble Steam Railway runs passenger services on its 1¼ mile (2km) line and hosts incoming rail tours. The Longridge, Knott End and Glasson Dock branches ran modest but regular services to Preston or Lancaster and occasionally beyond. Passenger services were discontinued on all three branch lines in 1930 due to the popularity of bus travel. The Whittingham Hospital branch ran about nine passenger trains daily, except on Sundays, that were free of charge to patients, staff and visitors alike. Trains connected with Longridge services until 1930 after which they were retimed to connect with the local bus service to/from Preston until final closure of the line in 1957. The Lancaster Old Goods line was exactly that since the L&CR took over management of the L&PJR in 1849, although the line did host the Ribble - Lune rail tour in 1964. Neither the St. George's Quay nor the Lancaster Power Station branches ran passenger services.

↑ *Bradshaw*, December 1902   ↑ Temperance hotel advert. (Preston Digital Archive)

↑ *Bradshaw*, January 1901   ↓ *Bradshaw*, December 1870

1. Fishergate Hill (Goods)

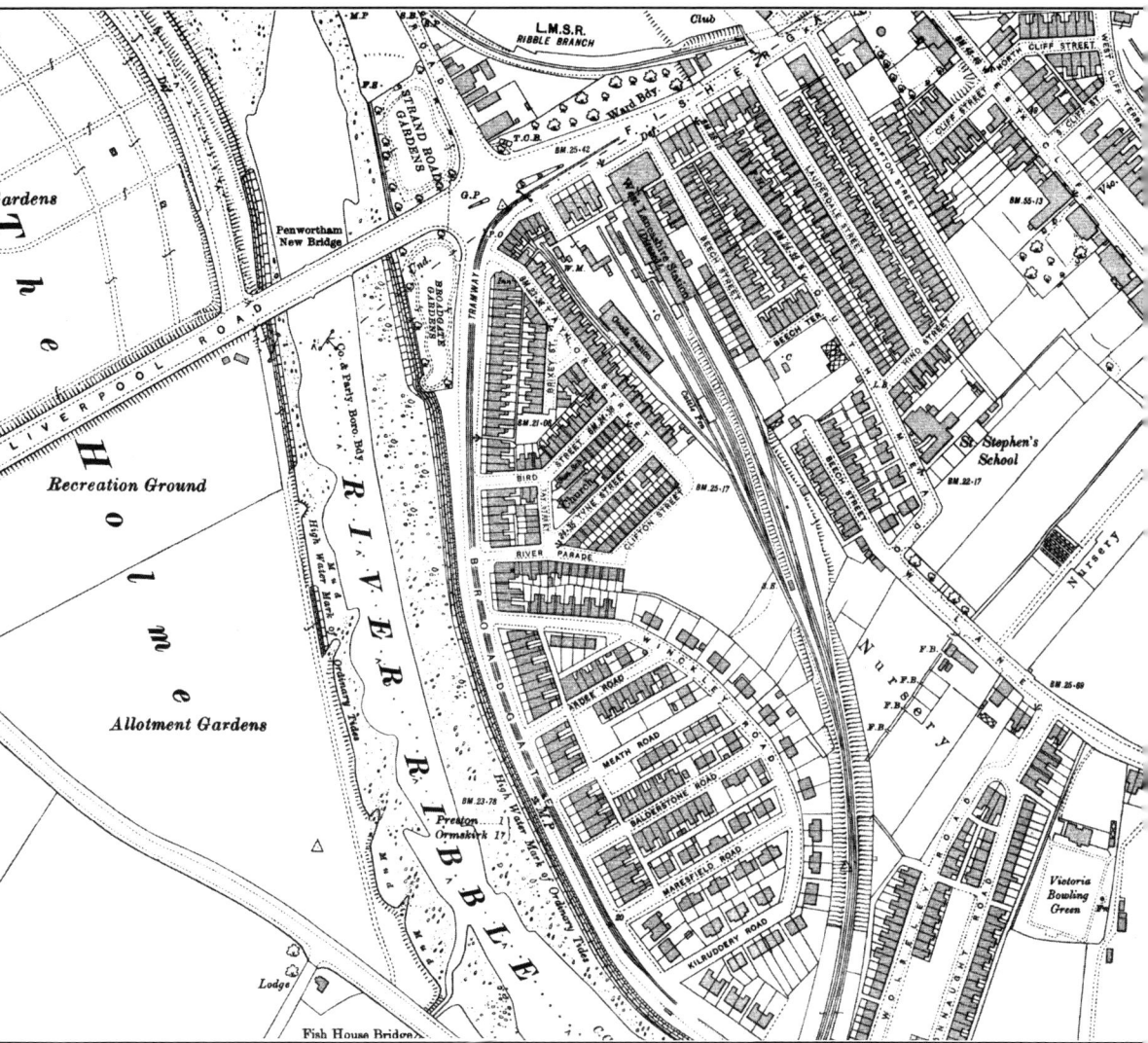

II. This 1937 map shows the former West Lancashire Railway station at Fishergate, Preston, which opened on 15th September 1882 and closed to passengers after only 18 years on 6th September 1902. The WLR was acquired by the L&YR in 1897 and thereafter passengers used Preston's East Lancs station. Fishergate remained open for goods and occasional specials during the Preston Guild festivals until final closure on 25th January 1965. In 1914, plans were made for two extensions of the WLR: [1] a spur to Preston docks along the alignment of Strand Road and joining the Ribble Branch where it crossed the road, thus avoiding the steep gradient down from Preston station and [2] an ambitious proposal to build a high-level line passing through the site of Fishergate joining the existing Blackpool line at Lea. The line would have avoided Preston and was ambitious by the fact that such a scheme would have required a second 'Penwortham bridge' crossing the Ribble downstream. Both projects were abandoned with the outbreak of WWI.

1. This is a view of the former West Lancashire Railway Terminus around 1965. Note that the central island platform has been removed.
(Preston Digital Archive)

→ 2. Ex-LNWR Beames 7F class G2 0-8-0 no. 49451 was ready to propel 1X23 RCTS Mid Lancs Railtour from Fishergate Hill on 22nd September 1962 to Penwortham Junction, where it reversed at Penwortham Ground Frame so the engine would then be leading as it headed towards Preston and on to Longridge. After Penwortham the tour continued to Whitehouse West Junction, Whitehouse South Junction, Todd Lane Junction, Lostock Hall, Farington Curve Junction

2. Preston Dock (Ribble) Branch

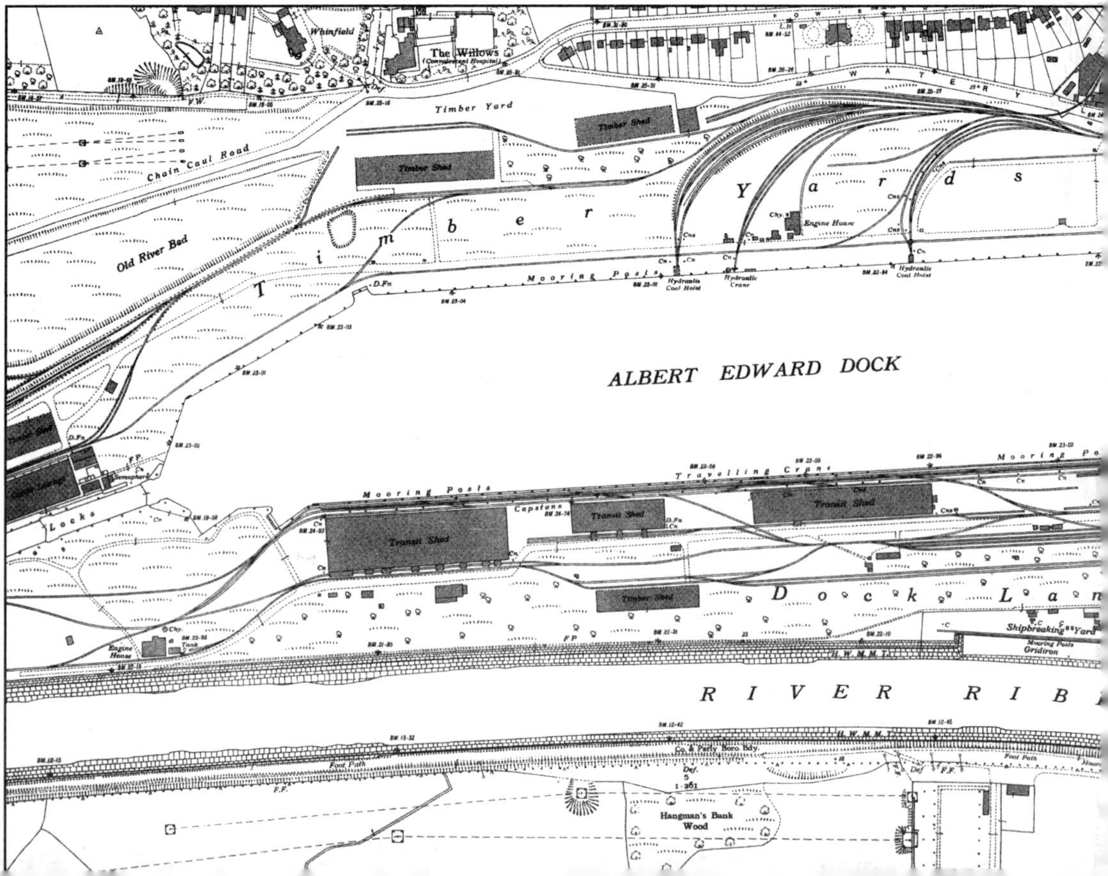

and Preston, after which it headed towards Longridge. The locomotive was withdrawn some two months later. After modification of the class the locomotives became known as 'Super Ds'. (Noel Machell)

III. This 1930 map shows the extensive rail network set up around the port together with the rail-served Dick, Kerr & Co works seen in the upper right of the map.

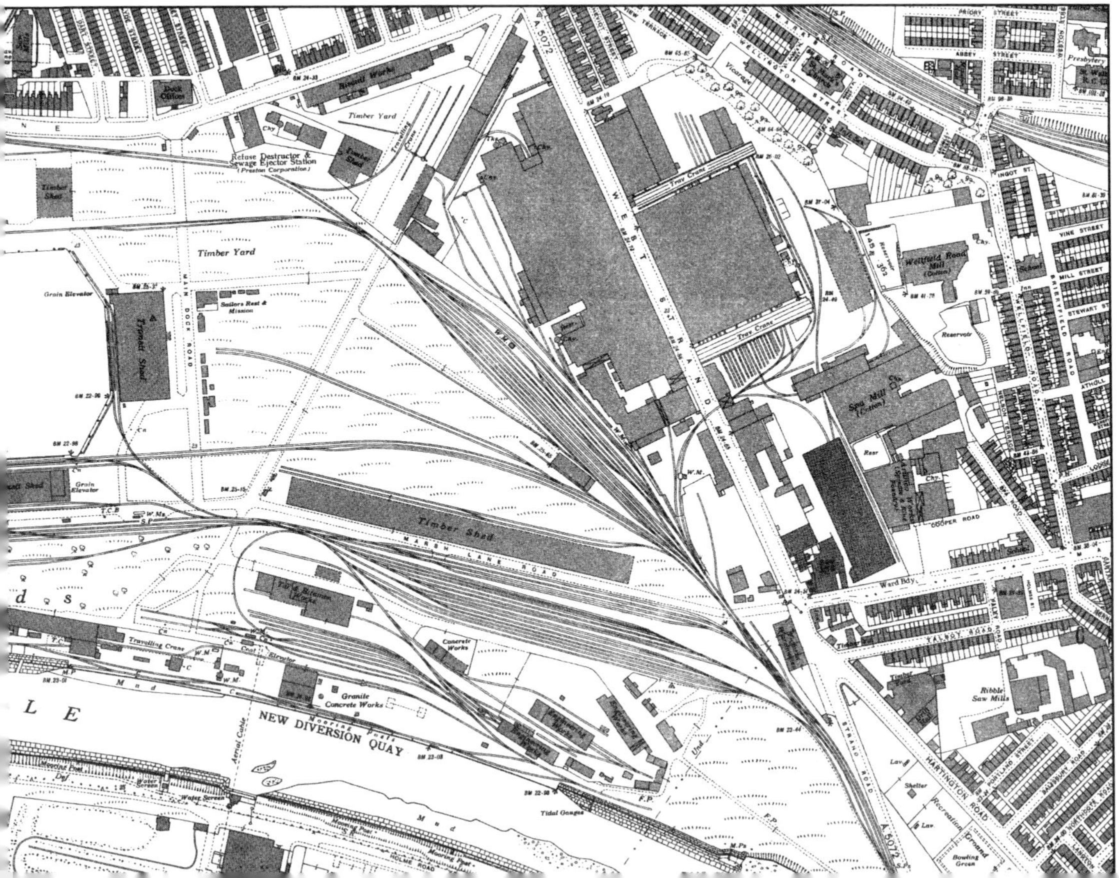

3. Although undated, this aerial view of Preston docks illustrates the railway infrastructure already in place as shown in Map III and is possibly of a similar date.
(G.Biddle collection/Kidderminster Railway Museum)

Branch Line to the Port

4. Ex-LMS Stanier class 8F 2-8-0 no. 48323 is seen passing Preston no. 2A signal box hauling a rake of chlorine tanks on 4th September 1967. The box straddled the Ribble Branch (Dock) line just south of the station, which descended down under Fishergate Hill and then crossed Strand Road and into the docks complex. (Lens of Sutton Association/John Faulkner collection)

5. View from the cab of GM Direct Rail Services class 66 Co-Co diesel locomotive no. 66432 leading the Branch Line Society 'Cat & Dock' tour on 15th June 2017 towards the fearsome looking 1:29 down to the dock alongside Preston station to the right. BR Sprinter class 150 no. 150112 is standing at platform 1 with the 12.23 from Manchester Victoria to Blackpool North.
(Geoff Plumb/Branch Line Society)

6. On the same day, again a view from the cab of no. 66432 as the train approaches the 140yd (128m) Fishergate Hill Tunnel and on towards the Strand Road level crossing. (Geoff Plumb/BLS)

7. Reportedly due to industrial action at Southampton Docks this Freightliner service was diverted to Preston and is seen here on 2nd April 1981 approaching the Strand Road crossing after exiting the Fishergate Hill tunnel behind English Electric type 4 1Co-Co1 class 40 no. 40191. Interestingly, after departure from the port the next day no. 40191 failed on the steep climb up to the main line and sister class 40 no. 40170 came to the rescue of the failed locomotive and its train. (John Matthews)

8. On 9th April 1992 BR Brush Type 4 class 47 Co-Co diesel locomotive no. 47277 is seen crossing Strand Road with bitumen tanks from Lindsey Oil Refinery at Immingham. Today traffic is much better controlled by half barriers at the crossing. (Peter Smith)

Port of Preston

9. Preston Corporation's William Bagnall 0-6-0ST works no. 2839 of 1946 *Perseverance* is seen here at the port in 1961 with a train of banana vans. Note the spark arrester on the chimney. (Peter Fidczuk collection)

10. Bagnall 0-6-0ST works no. 2893 built in 1945 *Conquerer* seen here in the mid-1960s passing under the grain elevator. (Gordon Edgar)

11. Andrew Barclay 0-6-0 fireless loco, works no. 1934 of 1927, *Duke*, is seen here exiting the Lancashire Tar Distillers complex with a train of Esso 14T bitumen tank wagons during the 1960s. (Peter Fidczuk collection)

12. The port of Preston's Armstrong Whitworth 0-6-0 diesel-electric works no. D8 of 1932 *Duchess* worked at the port in the mid-1960s. Originally the manufacturer's 'demonstrator loco' it was loaned to the London and North Eastern Railway and later the Southern Railway in 1932. Further trials followed with the Hartley Main railway, Lever Brothers at Port Sunlight and finally Ribble Navigation at Preston, which decided to purchase the shunter in 1935, where it worked alongside the Bagnall fleet until its withdrawal in 1969 coinciding with the arrival of the new Sentinel diesels. (Gordon Edgar)

13. This unidentified Preston Corporation William Bagnall 0-6-0ST is seen here on 20th September 1967 pulling away from the dockside. Spark arresters were fitted to most Bagnalls at the port as they often handled timber and wood pulp that was to be found in most of the sheeted wagons. (Preston Digital Archive)

14. 'PC' wagons on the quay sidings in late 1980. It is most likely that the two letters stood for Preston Corporation; note also on the ship's funnel the Preston coat of arms, the Lamb of St Wilfred, who is the patron saint of the city. (John Matthews)

15. A scene recording ICI Mond Division chlorine tanks on 10th January 1981. The Mond Division contained ICI's general chemicals operations. (John Matthews)

16. On 4th March 1981 a single BR English Electric Type 3 class 37 Co-Co diesel locomotive no. 37132 is seen near the GEC/EE factory, instead of the usual pair of Type 3s; it prepares to depart the yard with its empties. Coming into shot are the Rolls Royce Sentinel 0-4-0 diesel mechanical shunters, possibly no. 10281 *Energy* and no. 10282 *Enterprise* working a train of loaded tanks.
(John Matthews)

17. Further PC wagons that appear to be stored out of use, as was much of the dock at that time in late 1981. (John Matthews)

18. The loco is 0-4-0 Sentinel, works no. 10281 of 1968, *Energy*, one of three supplied to Preston Corporation for operating in the dock complex seen outside its shed in February 1992. The shed was retained by Preston City Council as a workshop for other council equipment and the Ribble Steam Railway (RSR) boundary ends within sight of it. The headshunt ends more or less where the Sentinel is standing. (Bill Roberton)

Thomas Ward

➔ 19. Thos. W. Ward Ltd was a Sheffield steel, engineering and cement business that began as coal and coke merchants and expanded into recycling metal for the city's steel industry and later manufacture and supply of machinery. In 1894 Ward ventured into ship breaking at various locations throughout the UK, one of which was at Preston Dock; until 1930 Ward had facilities at the stone jetty in nearby Morecambe. This is a view of Thos. Ward's Robert Stephenson & Hawthorn 0-4-0ST at its facility in February 1961. (Preston Digital Archive)

➔ *Promotional material. (Preston Digital Archive)*

Ribble Steam Railway and Museum

20. Bitumen tankers in the sidings near the Lancashire Tar Distillers and Totalfina plants at Preston Dock in 1992. The RSR and its museum occupy land to the left of the sidings and the line on which the tankers are residing is now occupied by the station platform. The line trailing off to the right runs to the Preston Corporation shed where the Sentinels were housed and maintained - see picture 18. (Bill Roberton)

21. After crossing Strand Road, seen on the right on 15th June 2017, the line heads west towards Preston Dock. The gates are supported on rather grand posts that date back to early days of rail operations at the port. (Geoff Plumb/BLS)

22. Ribble Steam Railway's William Bagnall 0-6-0ST no. 2680 *Courageous*, built in 1942 and restored to represent a Preston Dock locomotive, heads past the exchange sidings used for the bitumen traffic and running alongside Navigation Way on 11th September 2016. The spire of St Walburge can be seen in the distance. (Gordon Edgar)

23. There is something captivating about seeing very old machinery at work and they do not come much older than Sharp Stewart 0-4-0 tender locomotive Furness Railway no. 20 in FR Indian Red livery, which celebrated its 150th anniversary in 2013. The platform seen in this shot is built over what was the far left siding as shown in picture 20. (Mark Bartlett)

24. The year 2017 saw the 60th anniversary of the closure of the Whittingham Hospital Railway in 1957. To mark the occasion the Ribble Steam Railway museum had a small exhibition about the line as seen on 10th December 2017. In front is the resident Sentinel 0-4-0VBT (vertical boiler) *St Monans*, which is the same type as Whittingham Hospital Sentinel *Gradwell* used previously on the hospital railway. Alongside the locomotive is an elderly coach resembling one of those used on the same line. (Mark Bartlett)

25. Andrew Barclay 0-6-0ST no. 1833 of 1924 delivered as *Niddrie no. 6* of Niddrie and Benhar Coal Company but latterly NCB Lothian area no. 20 is seen here on 22nd May 2017 in the RSR workshop undergoing major works, including a virtually new boiler and repaired firebox. (Bill Roberton)

Ribble Steam Railway - Bitumen Services

The Ribble Steam Railway through its commercial freight subsidiary, Ribble Rail, handles all incoming and outgoing bitumen trains to and from the national network and the Total Energy Bitumen plant. It makes for a symbiotic relationship between the heritage railway and the incumbent freight operator.

↓ 26. BR Brush Type 5 class 60 Co-Co no. 60017 is in DBS livery arriving in the exchange sidings on 27th November 2013 with 14 bitumen tanks from Lindsey Oil Refinery at Immingham in Lincolnshire. At the time of the photograph the thrice-weekly service was routed via Manchester Victoria and Parkside due to the Copy Pit route being closed until March 2014. The train is running alongside empty tanks waiting to be returned to Lincolnshire. (Mark Bartlett)

↑ *An unidentified LNWR 0-8-0 freight locomotive lifts her safety valves in readiness for the short climb up the Ribble branch to Preston station seen here in around 1920 in the exchange sidings adjacent to Strand Road. (Preston Digital Archive)*

27. On 21st August 2009 visiting locomotive Barclay 0-6-0 shunter works no. 615 of 1977, on loan from the Tanfield Railway, is seen taking seven loaded wagons, the first of two such rakes, from the exchange sidings to the transfer sidings opposite the RSR station and museum. This was the last surface locomotive working for the National Coal Board. After 44 years of service, the ageing tank wagons were replaced in late 2010. (Mark Bartlett)

28. William Bagnall 0-6-0ST *Courageous* works hard with its 700-tonne loaded bitumen train over the Riversway swing bridge heading towards the transfer sidings on 3rd July 2017. The bridge provides access for river traffic to the Albert Edward basin. (Gordon Edgar)

29. Ribble Rail Sentinel 0-4-0 DM *Progress* shunts the second rake of seven tankers into the transfer sidings alongside the station and museum platform line on 22nd May 2017. (Bill Roberton)

30. This is the entrance to the bitumen processing plant seen from a passing RSR train on 6th February 2010. The plant is located at the far end of the tanks in the siding in picture 20 and is accessed from the transfer sidings opposite the platform as seen in the previous photograph. The unloading siding is only capable of holding seven tanks, which accounts for the transfer from the exchange sidings. The next morning the empties are tripped in two rakes to the exchange sidings. (Mark Bartlett)

Returning the Empties

31. Class 47 no. 47336 in Petroleum Sector livery is seen leaving the Preston Dock exchange sidings with 11 discharged bitumen tanks on the return service to Lindsey Oil Refinery on 21st May 1992. Note the hoarding announcing the Preston Guild Week of 1992. (Paul Shannon)

32. A class 66 hauls empty bitumen tanks up the 1:29 Preston Dock branch on the first stage of its journey back to Immingham. (Mark Bartlett)

Dick, Kerr & Co Works

Dick, Kerr & Co was formed in 1893 and its rail-served factory in Preston straddled Strand Road. It became a major centre of tram building and electrical equipment manufacture along with munitions in WWI. A major early railway contract awarded to the company in 1904 was for the electrification of the Liverpool Southport line of the L&YR. The company was acquired by English Electric in 1919, which much later merged with the General Electric Company plc. Among the factory's many achievements of the works there are two notables: [1] in 1955 it built the prototype Deltic locomotive and [2] the Dick, Kerr ladies football team.

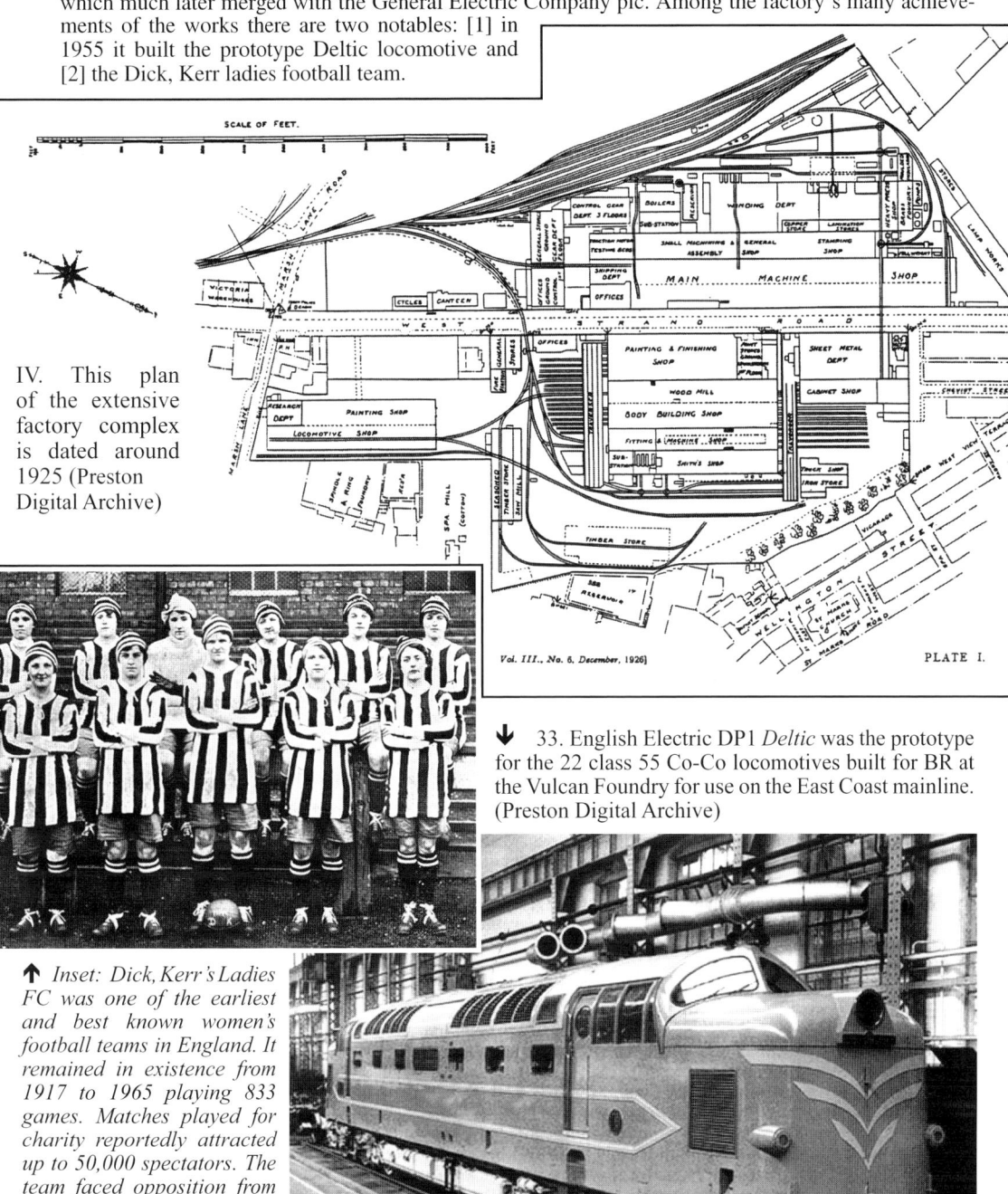

IV. This plan of the extensive factory complex is dated around 1925 (Preston Digital Archive)

↓ 33. English Electric DP1 *Deltic* was the prototype for the 22 class 55 Co-Co locomotives built for BR at the Vulcan Foundry for use on the East Coast mainline. (Preston Digital Archive)

↑ Inset: Dick, Kerr's Ladies FC was one of the earliest and best known women's football teams in England. It remained in existence from 1917 to 1965 playing 833 games. Matches played for charity reportedly attracted up to 50,000 spectators. The team faced opposition from the Football Association that later banned women's football for 50 years in the UK until 1971.
(Preston Digital Archive)

3. Preston & Longridge Railway
MAUDLAND

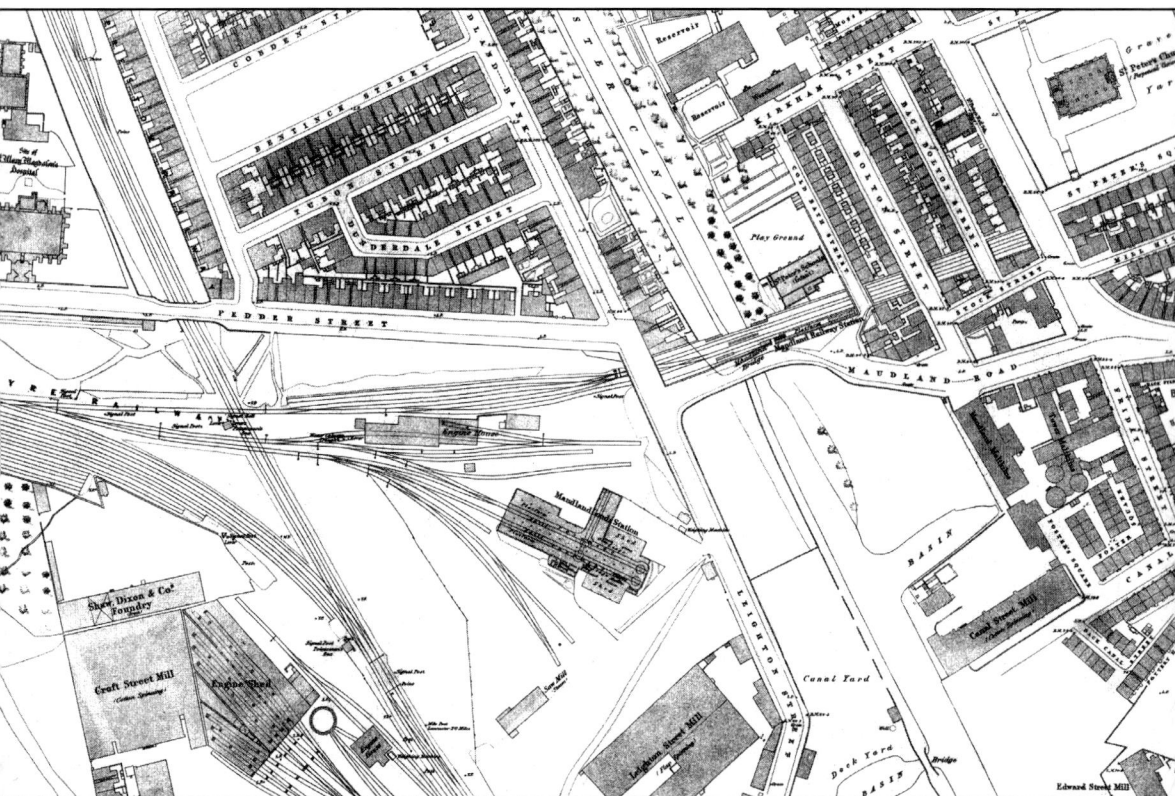

V. In this 1849 Town Plan the building shown as Maudland (Goods) station was the original terminus of the Preston & Wyre Railway at Leighton Street opened on 15th July 1840 and was reached by crossing the Lancaster & Preston Junction Railway (later to become the WCML) on the level. To the east of Leighton Street is Maudland Bridge station opened by the Fleetwood, Preston & West Riding Junction Railway on 1st November 1856 as the Preston terminus of the Preston & Longridge Railway. This map shows the end-on junction between the P&LR and P&WR just west of Maudland Bridge station, which was part of the failed attempt by the FP&WRJR to link Fleetwood with Leeds, Bradford and beyond.

➚ VI. By 1884 most of the P&WR trains ran into Preston main station. On 1st June 1885 Maudland Bridge station was closed and from then on P&LR trains also ran into the main station. Maudland Goods station can be seen on the right in picture 34.

➜ 34. A view across what was left of the Maudland goods yard and to the left the remaining link from the branch to the WCML taken on 2nd June 1978. Preston Power Box is straight ahead with its original flat roof, which leaked and was later replaced by a double hip-ended structure. Also seen is the then closed Penwortham Power Station on the south side of the River Ribble with its conveyor bridge and chimneys dominating the skyline. Class 47 no. 47429 heads towards Preston station with a Blackpool North to London Euston service whilst class 85 no. 85040 is stabled in the Croft Street Sidings. In the immediate foreground is a type VIX ferry van that was being loaded in the rather empty looking yard, although the goods shed was still standing. (Martyn Hilbert)

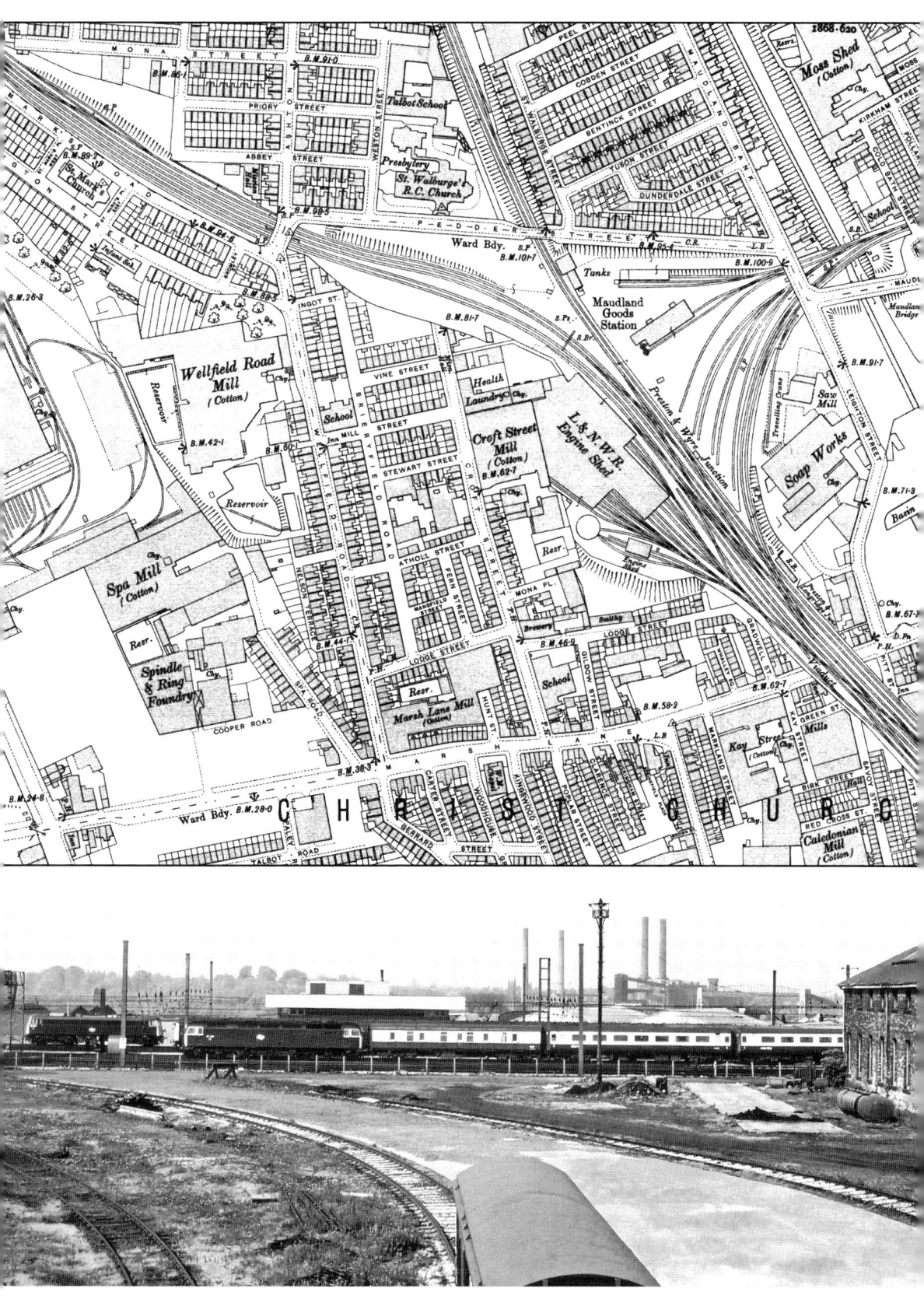

↑ 35. Maudland goods yard and shed taken on 10th January 1981 with a rake of vans waiting to be unloaded. Note the DMU in the background taking the Blackpool line. (John Matthews)

36. BR Sulzer Type 2 class 25 Bo-Bo diesel locomotive no. 25055, nicknamed Rats by enthusiasts, is seen exiting the now singled Miley Tunnel on 25th July 1979 passing the site of the former Maudland Bridge station and crossing the former route of the Lancaster canal. The impressive St Peter's church is seen in the background. (Tom Heavyside)

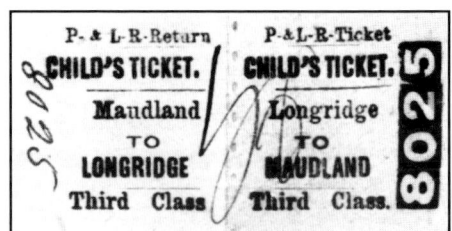

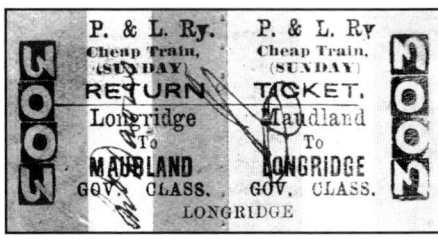

37. BR English Electric Type 4 class 40 1Co-Co1 no. 40186 is nearing the western end of Miley Tunnel on 7th June 1974 with empty mineral wagons from the Courtaulds Red Scar factory. (Thomas Sutch)

38. In this undated photo BR English Electric Type 2 class 20 Bo-Bo nos 20188 and 20121 double-head a train of 20T coal hoppers and a couple of cement wagons heading towards Deepdale from Walton Old Junction yard having just exited the Miley tunnel. (John Matthews)

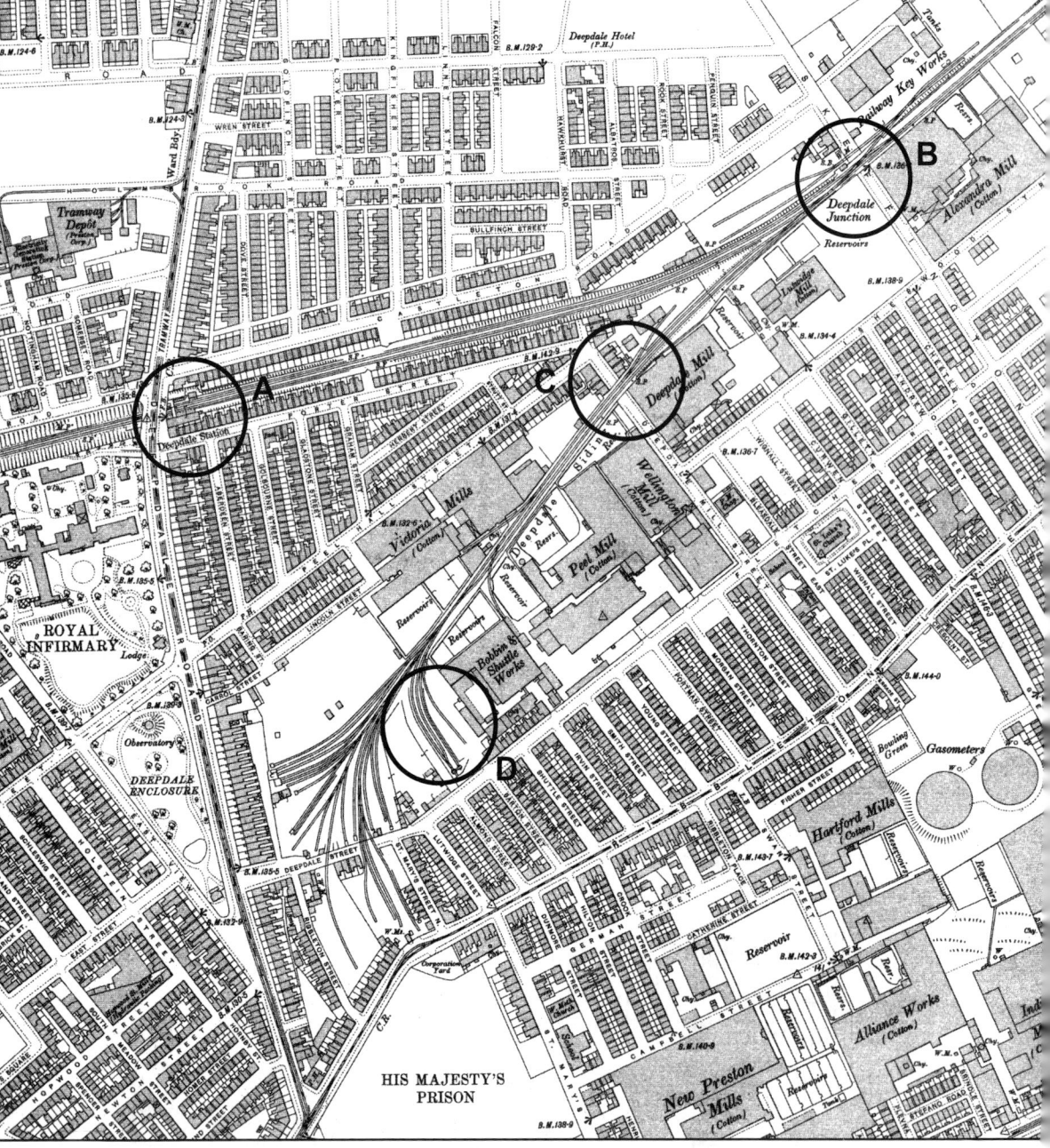

VII. This map shows the site of Deepdale station circled A, the Skeffington Road crossing B, Deepdale Mill Street Crossing C and the Deepdale coal concentration depot marked D.

➔ *Advertisement. (Preston Digital Archive)*

JOHN NOWELL,
Joiner, Builder, Wheelwright, Undertaker,
AND
GENERAL IRONMONGER,
201, Ribbleton Lane, Preston.
WORKS :—ANDREW STREET.

DEEPDALE

39. The rather unimposing entrance to Deepdale station on Deepdale Road as seen on 16th July 1964; some time after closure the premises became the Station Fruit Store. Opened by the FP&WRJR as Deepdale Bridge on 1st November 1856 and renamed Deepdale in 1867. (J.Marshall/Kidderminster Railway Museum)

40. The forlorn appearance of Deepdale station, which closed to passenger traffic in 1930, looking towards Preston on 1st May 1954.
(G.Biddle/Kidderminster Railway Museum)

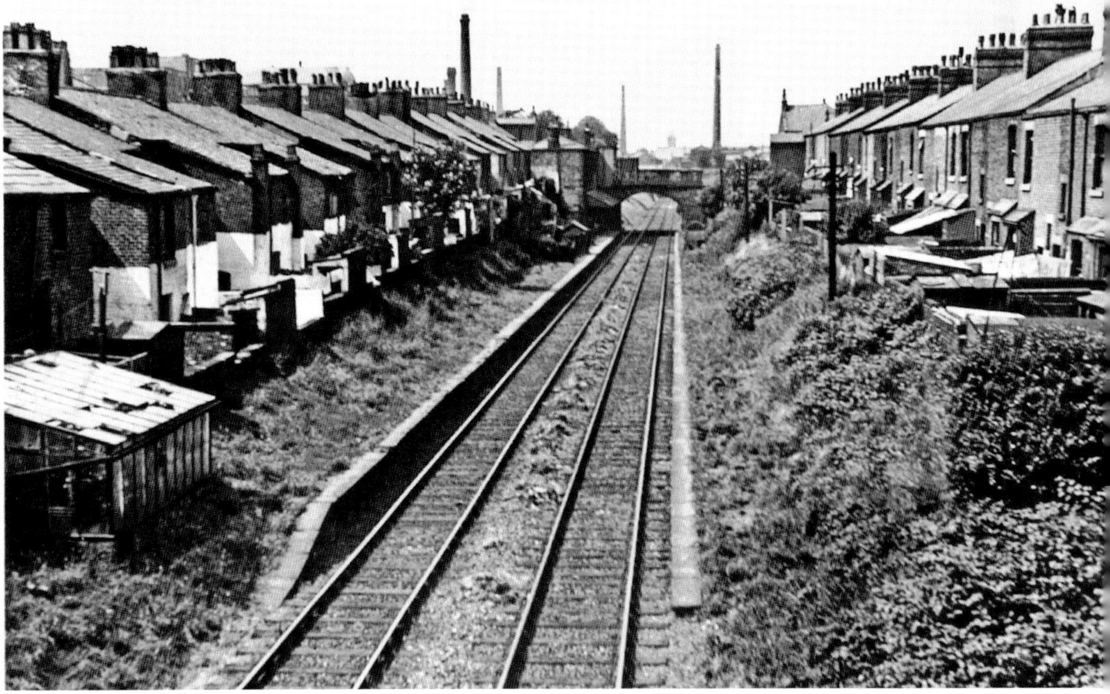

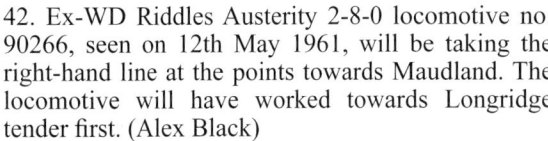

41. A view of an overgrown Deepdale station looking towards Maudland on 25th July 1949 taken from the intermediate footbridge linking Castletown Road and Porter Street. (John Alsop)

P & L R
EXCESS TICKET.
Deepdale Goods
To
from to Class.
Amount Paid

42. Ex-WD Riddles Austerity 2-8-0 locomotive no. 90266, seen on 12th May 1961, will be taking the right-hand line at the points towards Maudland. The locomotive will have worked towards Longridge tender first. (Alex Black)

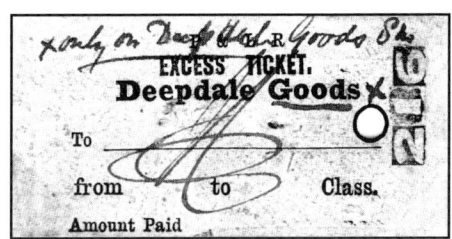

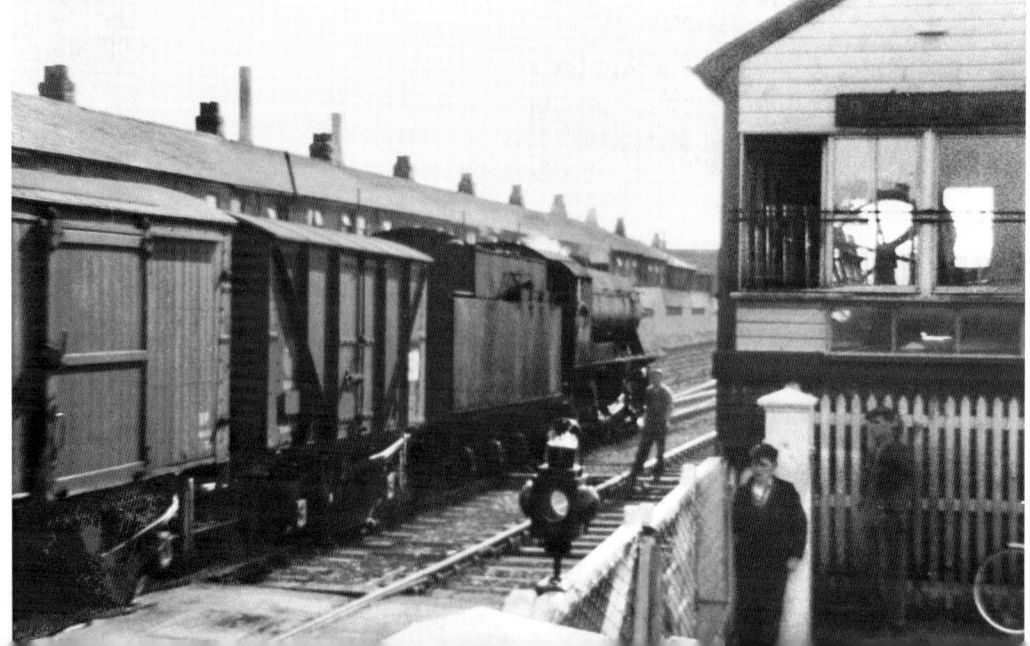

43. An unidentified class 40 shunts its train at Deepdale Junction in January 1980. (John Matthews)

↓ *Deepdale Mill Street level crossing seen on 16th July 1964. The crossing keeper's house this side of the gates was derelict for many years and has since been demolished. (J.Marshall/ Kidderminster Railway Museum)*

44. Class 20 nos 20094 and 20080 set back towards Deepdale coal concentration depot after working the 11.15 departure from Warrington Walton Old Junction on 2nd August 1985. The load comprises 7 HEA hoppers with coal from Kellingley colliery. On the adjacent track are 19 empty hoppers that will form the return working to Warrington. (Paul Shannon)

45. Lostock Hall engine ex-LMS Fowler 0-6-0T 'Jinty' no. 47572 crossing Deepdale Mill Street with a train of empties from the Coal Yard in late 1961 or possibly early 1962. It would then proceed to Skeffington Road crossing where it would run round its train before going forward to Preston. This crossing seemed very popular with children over the years. (Alex Black)

46. Class 37 no. 37118, in Railfreight grey large logo livery, was propelling loaded HEA Coal Hoppers across Deepdale Mill Street towards the coal depot on nearby Fletcher Road on a damp 17th July 1987. The cast-iron 'Beware of Trains' sign on the gate post was a rare survivor even in 1987. The photographer's car was an Escort Bravo limited edition. (Martyn Hilbert)

DEEPDALE STREET

47. Deepdale Street station was the original western terminus of the P&LR. It opened on 1st May 1840 and is seen here on 25th July 1949 some time before 20T hoppers were seen at the yard. The station closed to passengers on 1st November 1856, when the line was diverted via Deepdale and the Miley Tunnel to the new station at Maudland Bridge. Originally stone from the Longridge quarries would have been brought to the sidings at Deepdale Street and it was those sidings that were used later for coal distribution and cement traffic. (Robert Humm coll.)

48. A 1976 view of 1887-built Wigan Coal & Iron Company 0-6-0ST *Lindsay* languishing since 1968 in the Maudland Metals scrapyard located alongside the Deepdale coal depot. It was purchased in 1976 by the Lindsay Loco Trust and subsequently used at Steamtown, Carnforth, where it was presented in an Indian red livery. Later it was stored out of use at the West Coast Railway's depot and in October 2019 it was acquired by Mr James Bunch and taken to a private location for restoration to working order. (Gordon Edgar)

49. Having arrived from Warrington Arpley Yard on 12th April 1985 with loaded coal hoppers, class 25/2 no. 25181 had propelled them into the coal concentration depot. The empty hoppers would have been winched out of the yard by rope and capstan allowing the class 25 to be backed on to the wagons and push them backwards towards Deepdale Junction for the return journey to Warrington. The yard saw its last coal train in 1997. (Martyn Hilbert)

Ministry of Supply warehouse

50. In this undated picture taken from the Cromwell Road bridge, circled on map VIII, an unidentified ex-L&YR Aspinall 0-6-0 is seen hauling coal wagons for Courtauld's Red Scar factory passing the Ministry of Supply warehouse and cold store. OS maps dating from pre-1945 were censored and the Ministry building is not shown. The area is the site of the Battle of Preston in 1648 that resulted in a victory for the New Model Army under the command of Oliver Cromwell. (David Hindle)

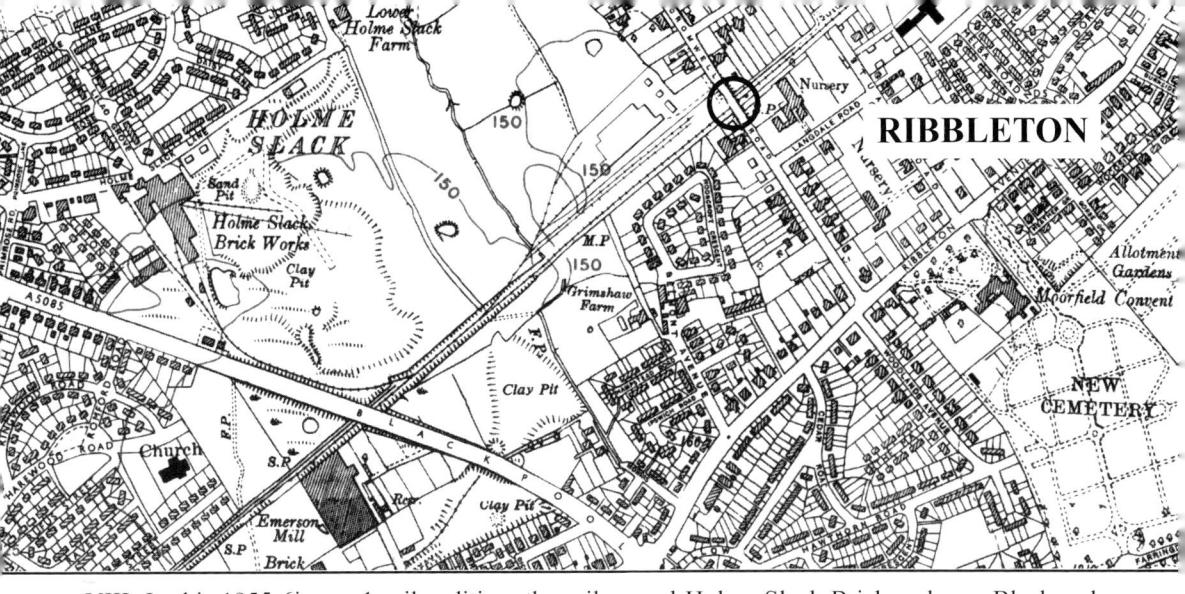

RIBBLETON

VIII. In this 1955 6ins to 1 mile edition, the rail-served Holme Slack Brickworks on Blackpool Road is clearly marked. In the top right is a rail-served cold store. Deepdale Retail Park is built on the site of the former brick works.

IX. When Ribbleton station opened in 1854 it was called Gamull Lane; any reference to Gammer Lane appears to be a misprint in the timetable. The line through the station continued to be used for goods trains to and from Courtaulds Red Scar Works until its closure in 1980 after which the line was cut back to a headshunt to the east of Skeffington Road crossing. In 1856 the station name was changed from Gammer Lane to Fulwood and in 1900 to Ribbleton. The station was closed on 31st May 1930. After closure of the line, the Gamull Lane overbridge was removed and the route on either side is now a combined cycle path and footpath that now passes behind the station building. The building still stands; it was a private house with the former trackbed running through its garden until it was bought by Preston Trampower in 2021 with the intention of using it as their headquarters.

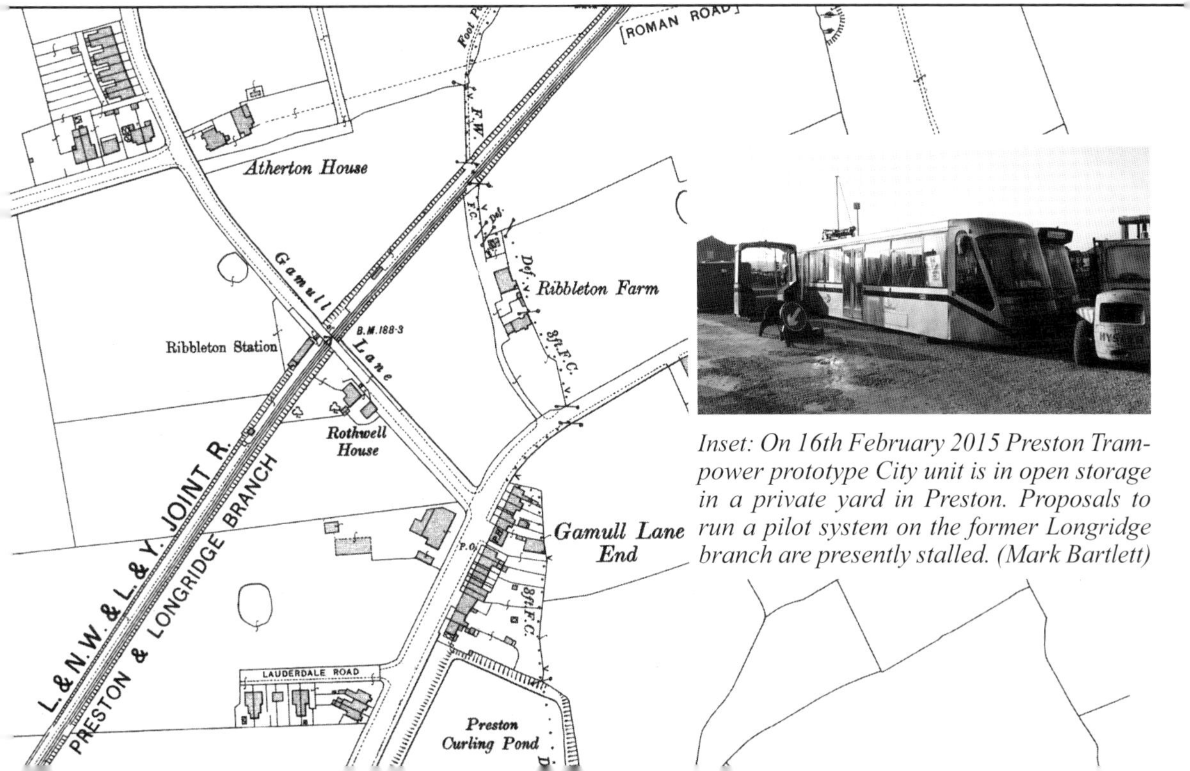

Inset: On 16th February 2015 Preston Trampower prototype City unit is in open storage in a private yard in Preston. Proposals to run a pilot system on the former Longridge branch are presently stalled. (Mark Bartlett)

51. Back on the line to Longridge, taken on 1st May 1954, is a shot of the former and short-lived station called Ribbleton that opened in 1863 and closed in 1866. The short platform saw occasional use after closure with troop specials for the nearby Fulwood Barracks. The other station at Gamull Lane was not named Ribbleton until 1900.
(G.Biddle/
Kidderminster Railway Museum)

➔ X. Beyond Ribbleton station - seen bottom left - this 6ins to 1 mile map of 1955 shows the extensive rail-served Courtaulds Red Scar Rayon Works. The factory had its own power station hence the coal trains and other raw materials brought in by rail included sulphuric acid, sodium hydroxide, carbon disulphide and wood pulp. Closure of the factory was announced in November 1979; it closed the following year and was demolished in 1982.

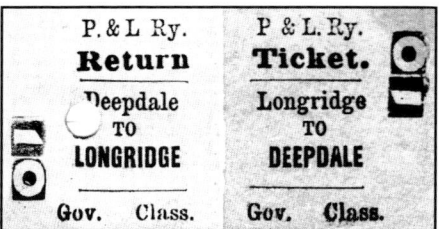

52. A busy scene at the second Ribbleton station in September 1911. The bridge at the far end of the platform carried Gamull Lane over the line. The station was renamed Fulwood in 1856 and Ribbleton in 1900. (John Alsop)

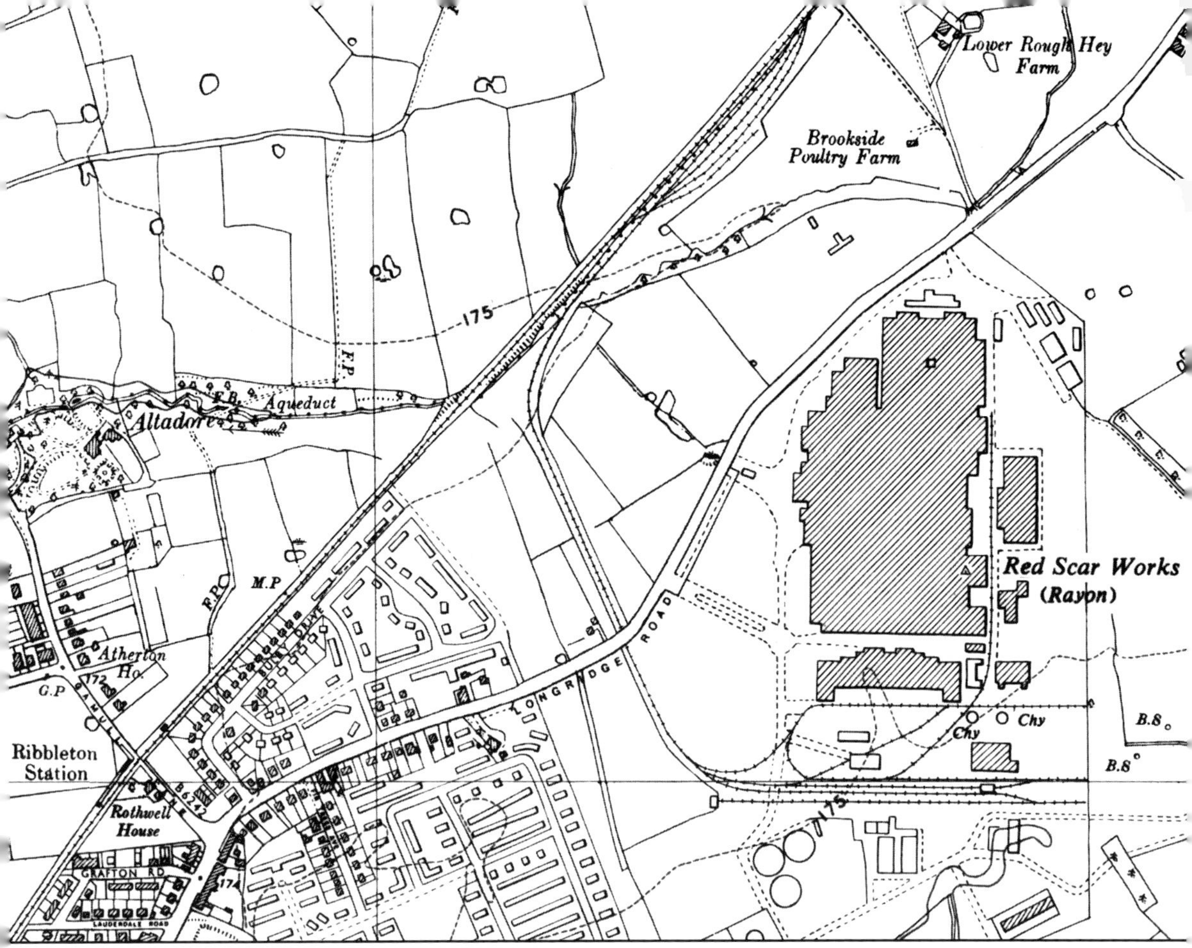

⬇ 53. Seen on shed on 21st November 1966 are Peckett 0-4-0ST locomotives at the Red Scar factory. To the fore is works no. 1925 *Caliban*, built in 1937, now preserved at the Ribble Steam Railway. Behind is works no. 2087 *Miranda*, built in 1948 for Courtaulds Aber works in Flint. Originally named *Dafydd*, the latter was later transferred to Wolverhampton, where it lost the name. Finally it was transferred to Red Scar where it was rebuilt with parts from scrapped sister engine no. 2086 and named *Miranda*; it worked there until 1968. After several attempts at preservation the locomotive now resides at the Buckingham Railway Centre, where it bears the name *Gibraltar*. The two Pecketts were replaced by a Sentinel in 1967. (Michael Ellis)

54. The final coal train at Red Scar works is hauled by class 40 no. 40012 with loaded wagons from Wigan on 8th February 1980. (John Matthews)

GRIMSARGH

XI. This opened on 1st May 1840 although passenger facilities were lacking for some time and initially the nearby Plough Hotel, as seen in this map, was used as a booking office. However, in 1870 the station building, as seen in the photographs, was constructed by the line's joint owners, the LNWR and L&YR. The hospital line station had a run-around loop and an exchange siding with the Longridge line.

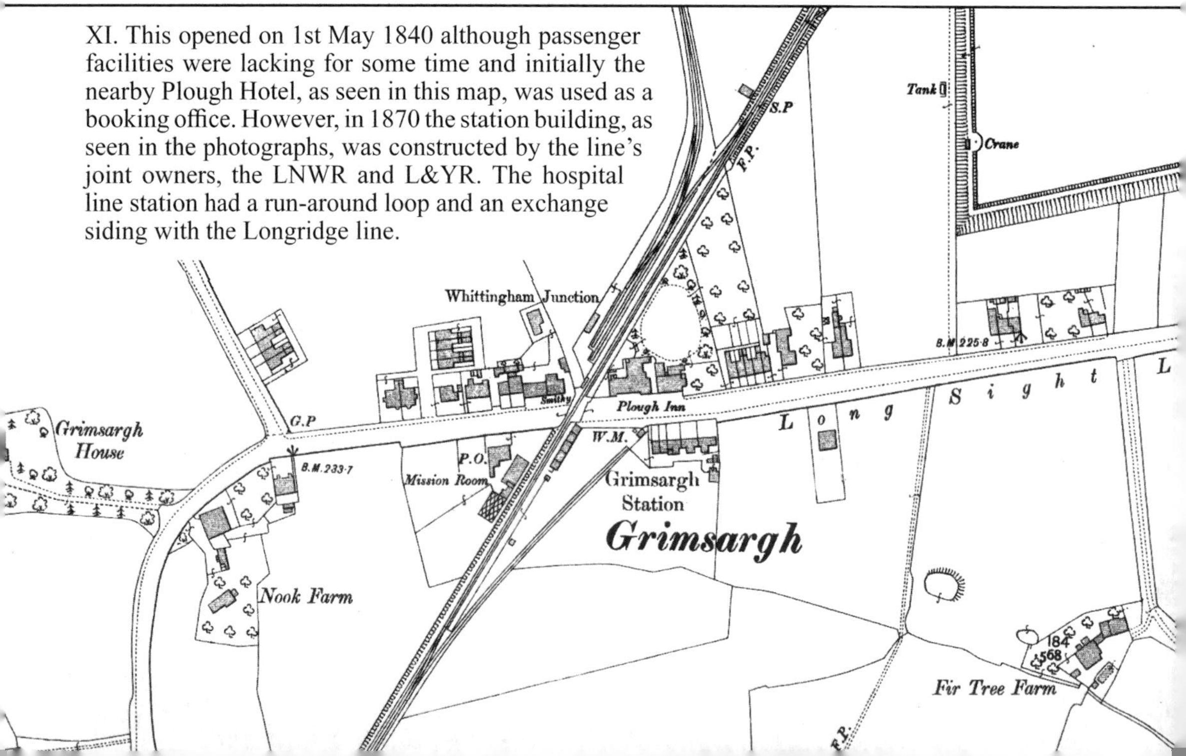

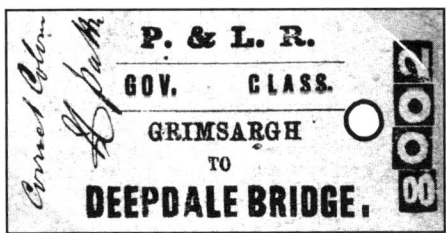

55. A very popular Grimsargh station seen in this post-1870 shot taken from the site of the Grimsargh hospital branch station and looking towards Preston. (Transport Treasury)

56. Grimsargh station and level crossing in 1964 looking towards Longridge with a view of the former Whittingham Hospital branch passenger station to the left. (Preston Digital Archive courtesy of Tony Gillett)

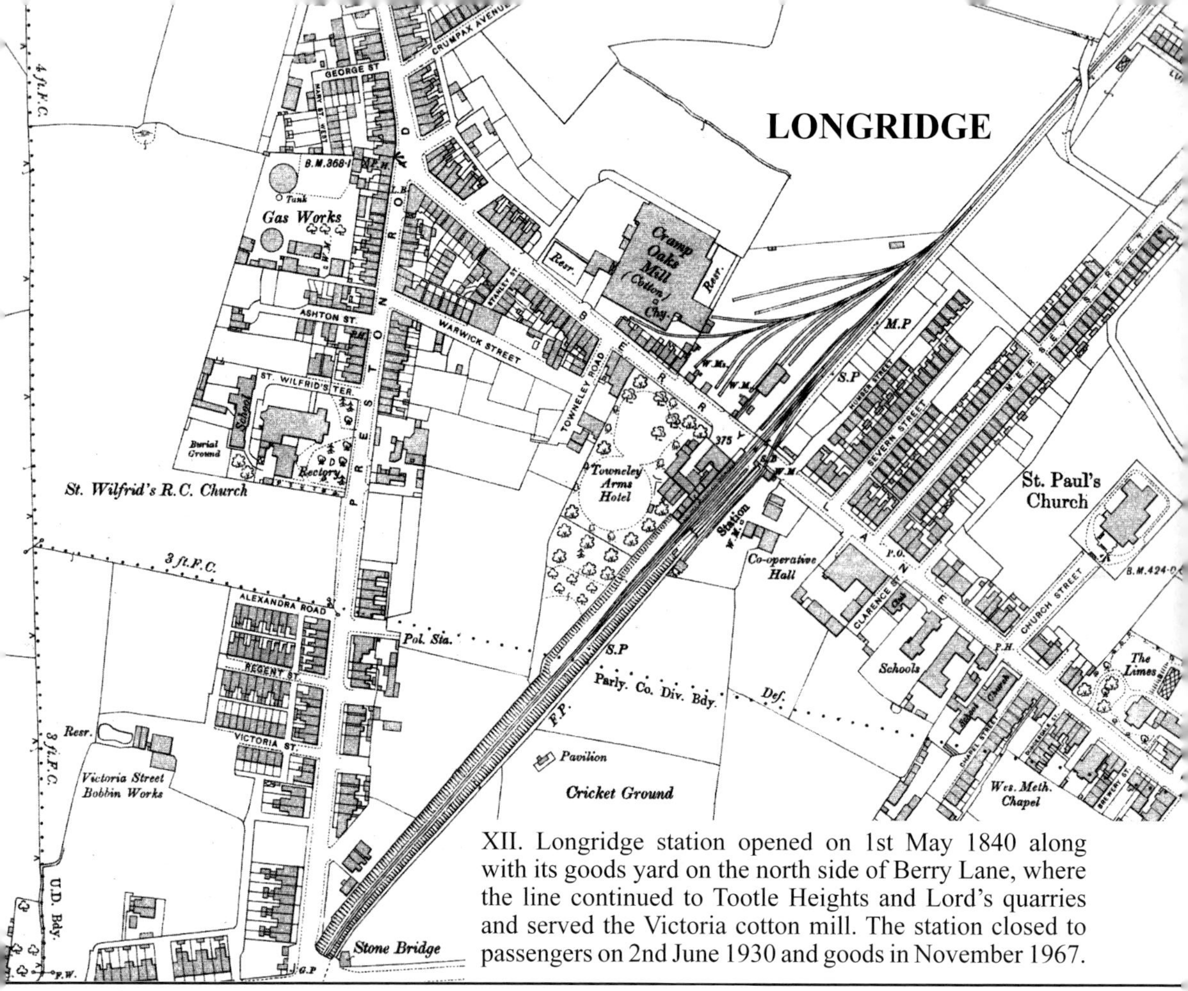

LONGRIDGE

XII. Longridge station opened on 1st May 1840 along with its goods yard on the north side of Berry Lane, where the line continued to Tootle Heights and Lord's quarries and served the Victoria cotton mill. The station closed to passengers on 2nd June 1930 and goods in November 1967.

57. A new LNWR motor train comprising an unidentified LNWR Webb class 1P 2-4-2T between two pairs of coaches is seen in 1914. The plaque above the window over the main entrance reads 'Longridge Cycling Club Headquarters'. (Lens of Sutton Association)

58. World War I army volunteers stand on Longridge station up platform in February 1915. (Lens of Sutton Association)

59. Once again we see the RCTS tour of lines not normally open for passenger traffic around East Lancashire and West Yorkshire on 22nd September 1962 see also picture no. 2. Here we see the Super D no. 49451 in the process of running round its train prior to returning to Preston tender first. The locomotive allocated to Springs Branch depot had been carefully cleaned and polished by the staff there and is seen at the Berry Lane level crossing with the signal box and the Towneley Arms Hotel in the background. (Noel Machell)

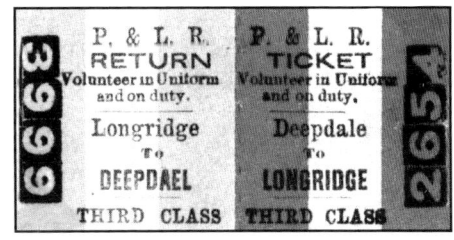

60. A view from track level at Longridge, where the line advances beyond the weigh bridge in the foreground towards the Tootle Heights quarry through the short tunnel seen in the distance on 5th August 1928. The lines were lifted around 1940. The tunnel entrance is Grade II listed.
(J.Ashworth/Kidderminster Railway Museum)

➔ An advert for the Bond lightweight Lilliput Motorcycle that debuted in 1951. The Bond Aircraft and Engineering Company was abbreviated by the owner to BAC but not to be confused with the British Aircraft Corporation also of Preston founded in 1960.
(Preston Digital Archive)

Introducing the new
"**B.A.C. LILLIPUT**"
98c.c. Lightweight
Amazing Performance and Economy

PRICE £52·10·0
PLUS £14.3.0 PURCHASE TAX
Manufactured by
BOND AIRCRAFT & ENG. CO. (B'POOL) LTD
TOWNELEY WORKS **LONGRIDGE**
LANCS   TEL. 3172

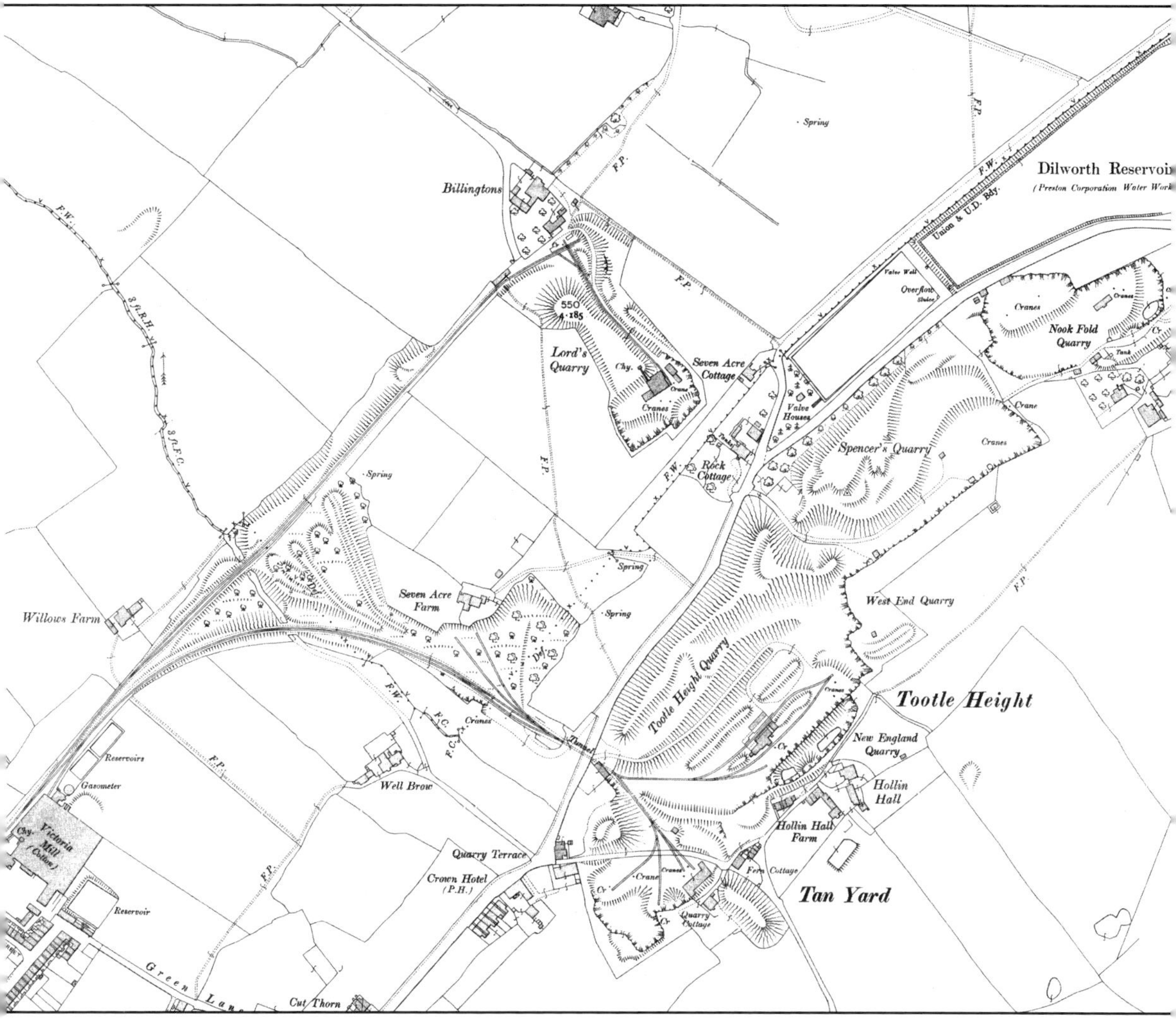

XIII. After passing the Longridge goods yard the line splits to serve the Tootle Heights and Lord's quarries.

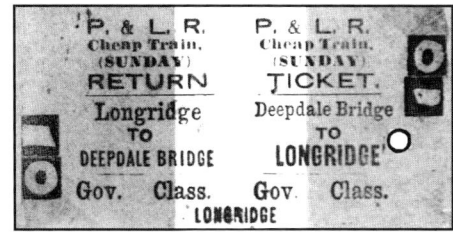

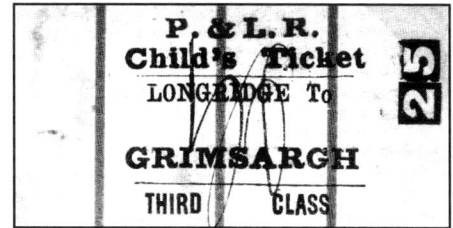

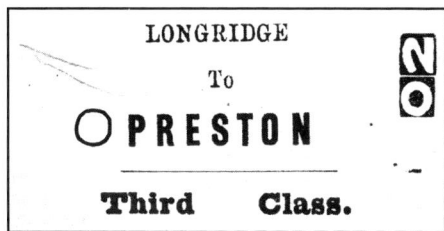

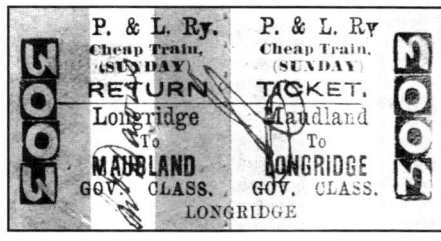

4. Whittingham Hospital Railway

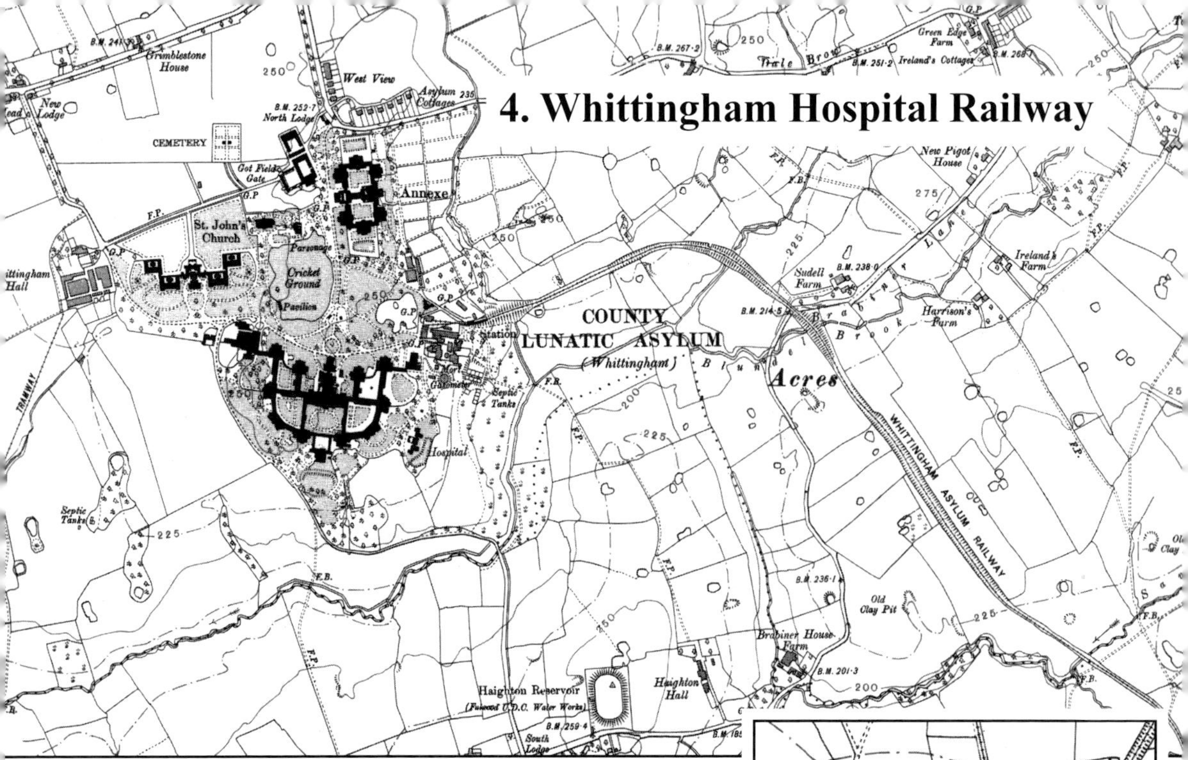

XIV. In this 6ins map of 1914 the 2 mile (3.2km) private line from Grimsargh to the psychiatric hospital at Whittingham is featured. The line was used to transport coal and other goods to the hospital and provided free travel for staff, patients and visitors. The hospital opened in 1873 and the railway some years later. Until 1930 the hospital trains connected with services on the Longridge branch until passenger traffic ceased; after that hospital services connected with Preston - Longridge bus services in Grimsargh village. The line closed on 30th June 1957 and the hospital in 1995. During the inter-war years it was the largest mental health hospital in the UK. The inset map, right, shows the junction with the Longridge line.

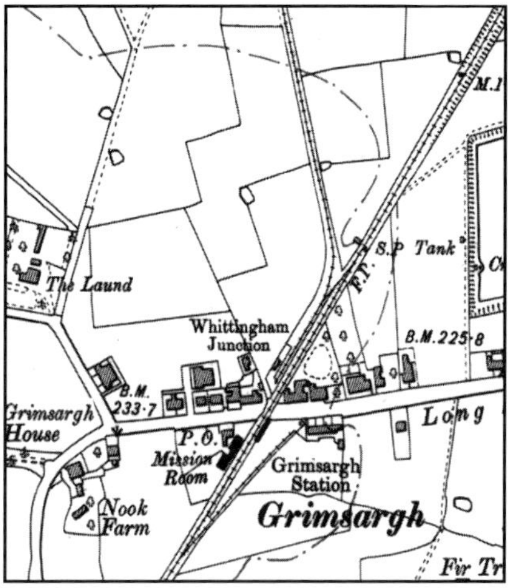

The main hospital entrance at St. Luke's Division taken in the 1950s. (Preston Digital Archive/Phil Knapman)

➜ 62. Sentinel 0-4-0 *Gradwell* is working a mixed traffic service in the hospital grounds. The three ex-LNWR brake vans had been converted in later years to become passenger stock. It made its last journey to Whittingham on 29th June 1957, the day before closure of the line.
(Peter Fidczuk coll.)

GRIMSARGH HOSPITAL HALT

↑ 61. Andrew Barclay 0-4-2T no. 2 purchased by the railway in 1904 is seen in the late 1920s waiting at the Grimsargh Hospital Platform before departing for Whittingham. The locomotive is hauling an interesting rake of coaches; the first two, both four-wheelers, are former L&YR and North London Railway vehicles and the third is possibly the coach purchased from the Lancaster Carriage and Wagon Works. Note the superb lamp on the station awning. (Edwin Ashworth/ Ron Herbert coll.)

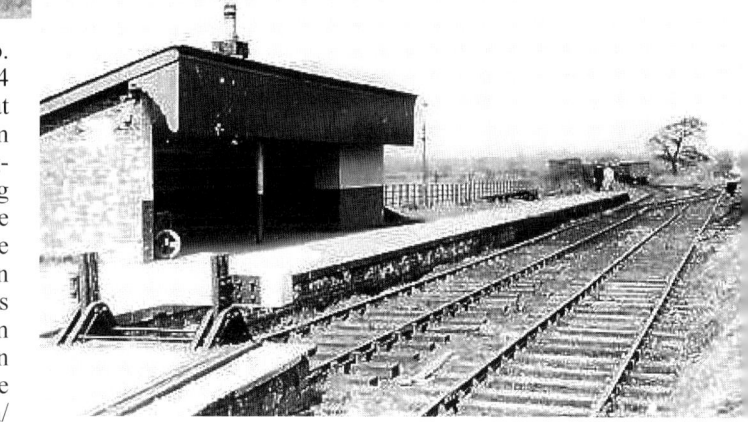

↑ *Grimsargh Hospital platform and shelter c1955. (Preston Digital Archive)*

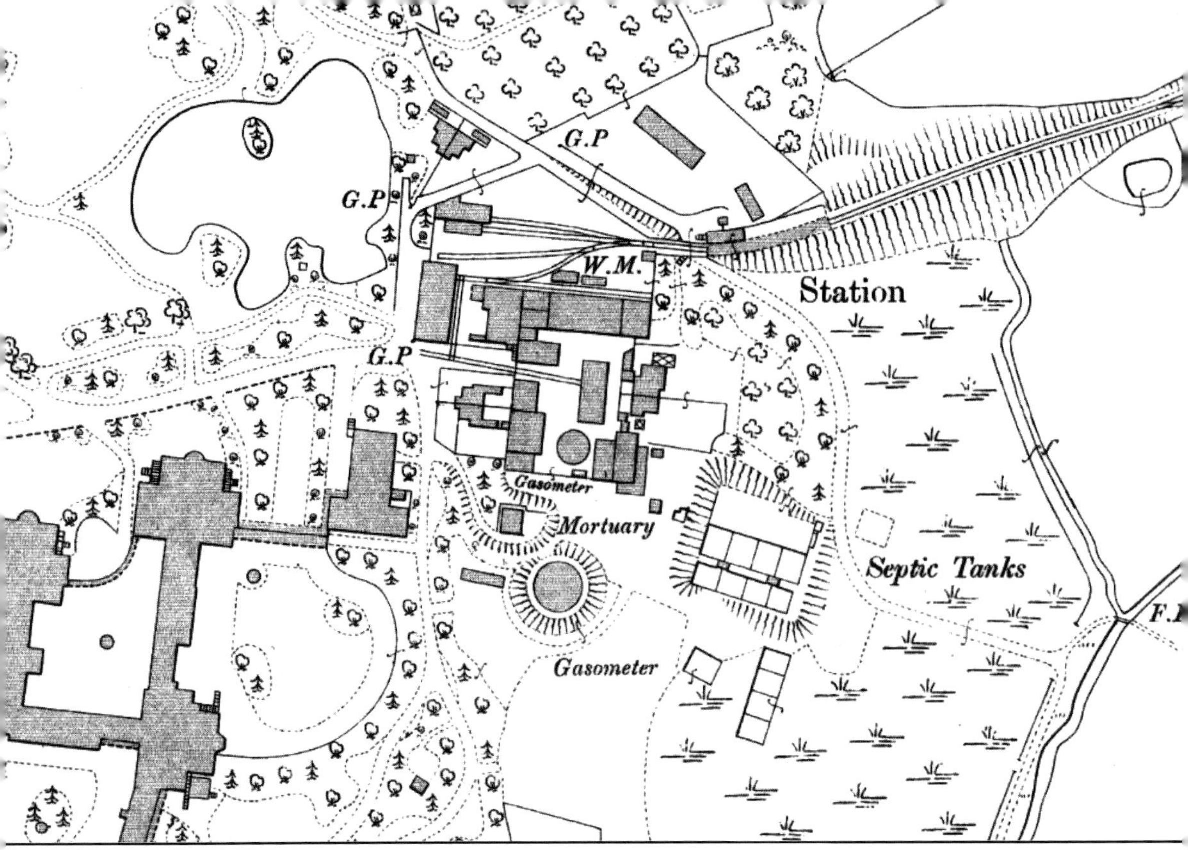

XV. A detailed look at the hospital railway layout in this extract, with the station to the right and goods facilities to the left.

63. A view of Whittingham railway yard and sheds in 1948. The engine shed is to the right with a wagon in the doorway and as recently as 2022 the building was still in use as an NHS workshop. (Preston Digital Archive/Phil Knapman)

WHITTINGHAM HOSPITAL

64. The line opened for freight in June 1889 and for passenger services not much later. In this undated shot viewed from the goods yard a train is waiting to depart on the 10 minute journey to Grimsargh. (John Alsop)

➔ *In 1923 the name 'Whittingham Asylum' was dropped in favour of 'Whittingham Mental Hospital'.*

Bradshaw, July 1924

	PRESTON and LONGRIDGE.—L. M. & S.														
Miles	**Down.**					**Week Days.**									
		mrn	mrn	mrn		E	S	E	S		aft	E	S	aft	aft	aft	aft	S	
	Preston..............dep.	6 0	7 59	10	....	1050	1130	1210	1235	....	1 58	3 45	aft	5 19	6 35	....	8 29	17	1025	....
1¼	Deepdale.............	6 5	7 10	9 15	....	1055	1135	1215	1240	....	2 3	3 50	4 15	5 24	6 40	....	8 7	9 22	1031	....
3¼	Ribbleton............	6 11	7 16	9 21	....	11 1	1141	1221	1245	....	2 9	3 56	4 20	5 30	6 46	....	8 13	9 28	1037	....
5	Grimsargh, for Whittingham...	6 17	7 22	9 27	....	11 7	1147	1227	1255	....	2 15	4 2	4 26	5 36	6 52	....	8 19	9 35	1042	....
7¼	Longridge............arr.	6 25	7 30	9 37	....	1119	12 0	1237	1 2	....	2 25	4 12	4 35	5 46.7	2	....	8 29	9 43	1052	....
Miles	**Up.**					**Week Days.**									
		mrn	mrn			mrn	E	S	E	S			S	E	aft	aft	aft	aft	S
	Longridge...........dep.	6 35	8 3	....	10 0	1130	1225	....	1 51	15 2	35	2 35	....	4 45	5 6	0 7	10 8	38 9	53	....	1110
2¼	Grimsargh, for Whittingham...	6 40	8 11	....	10 5	1135	1230	....	1 10	1 20	2 40	2 40	....	4 50	5 9	6 6	7 15	8 43	9 58	....	1115
4	Ribbleton............	6 44	8 18	....	10 9	1139	1234	....	1 14	1 24	2 44	2 44	....	4 54	5 13	6 10	7 19	8 47	10 2	....	1119
5¾	Deepdale......	473, **492**, 503	6 50	8 24	....	1015	1145	1240	....	1 20	1 30	2 50	2 50	....	5 0	5 19	6 17	7 25	8 53	10 8	....	1125
7¼	Preston **328**, **334**, **468**, arr.	6 57	8 34	....	1024	1152	1249	....	1 27	1 40	2 59	....	....	5 7	5 27	6 24	7 32	9 0	1015	....	1132
	Down.			**Sundays.**					**Up.**			**Sundays.**				
		mrn	mrn		aft	aft					mrn	mrn		aft	aft	
	Preston..............dep.	7 59	15	....	2 30	6 0	....		Longridge...........dep.	7 45	9 50	....	3 10	6 40	....
	Deepdale.............	7 10	9 20	....	2 35	6 5	....		Grimsargh, for Whittingham...	7 54	9 55	....	3 15	6 45	....
	Ribbleton............								Ribbleton............						
	Grimsargh, for Whittingham...	7 22	9 31	....	2 46	6 18	....		Deepdale...... 472, 477, 503	8 4	10 4	....	3 24	6 54	....
	Longridge............arr.	7 32	9 41	....	2 56	6 28	....		Preston **332**, **338**, **495**, arr.	8 11	1011	....	3 31	7 1	....
			E Except Saturdays.		**S** Saturdays only.										

5. Garstang & Knott End Railway
GARSTANG & CATTERALL

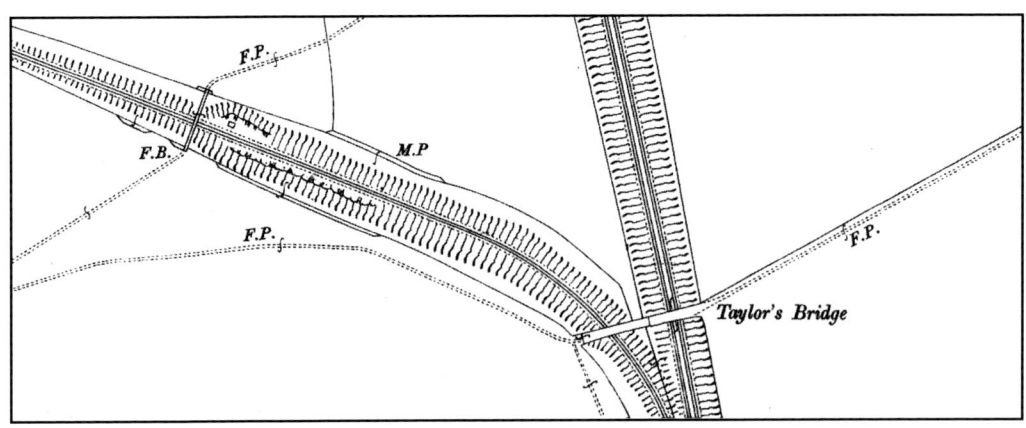

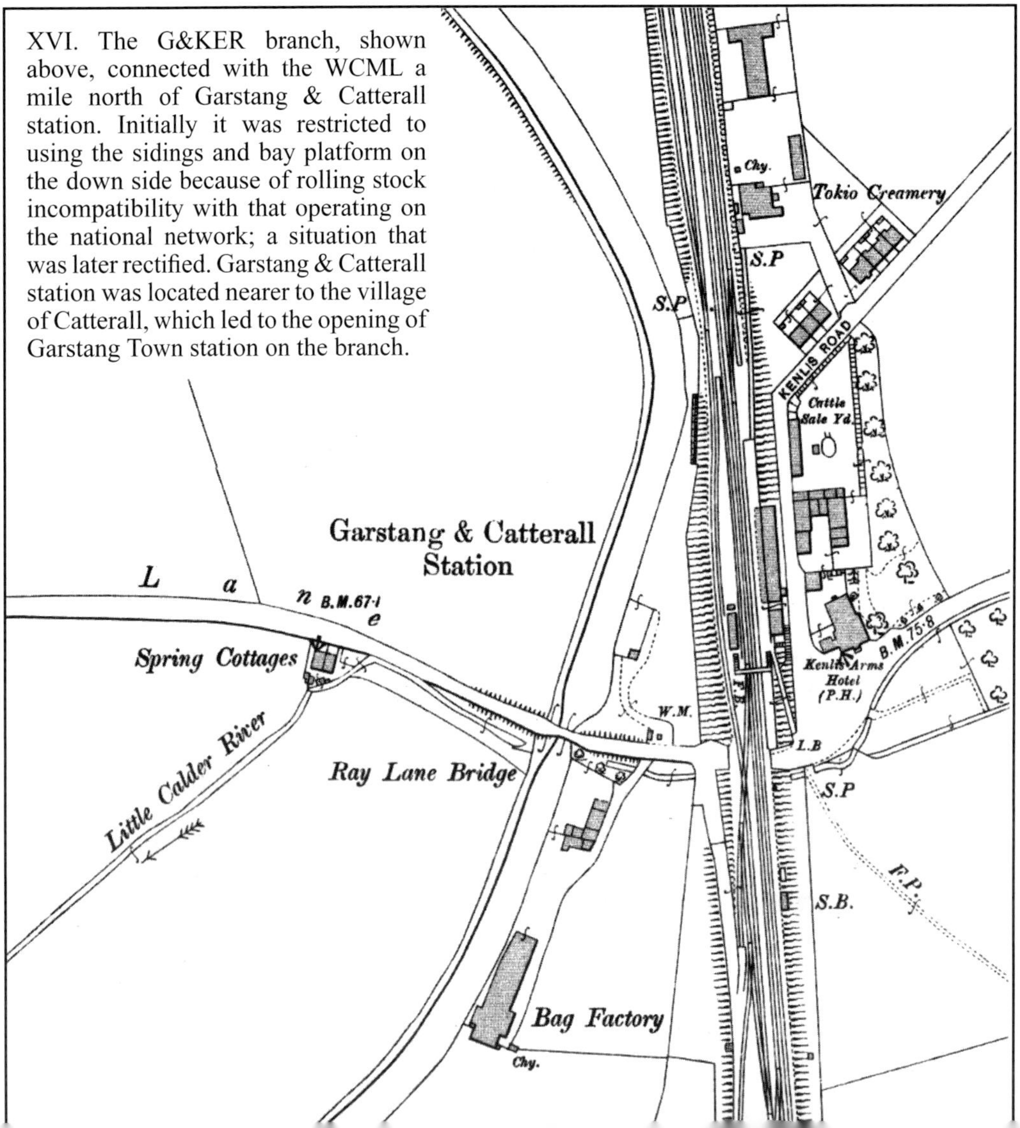

XVI. The G&KER branch, shown above, connected with the WCML a mile north of Garstang & Catterall station. Initially it was restricted to using the sidings and bay platform on the down side because of rolling stock incompatibility with that operating on the national network; a situation that was later rectified. Garstang & Catterall station was located nearer to the village of Catterall, which led to the opening of Garstang Town station on the branch.

65. Built in 1897 Hudswell Clarke 0-6-0ST *Jubilee Queen* is seen in the 'branch' platform at Garstang & Catterall looking towards Preston on 30th July 1912. (Robert Humm coll.)

66. A mixed G&KER freight also stands in the 'branch' platform under the charge of Hudswell Clarke 0-6-0ST *New Century* in around 1908. (Lens of Sutton Association)

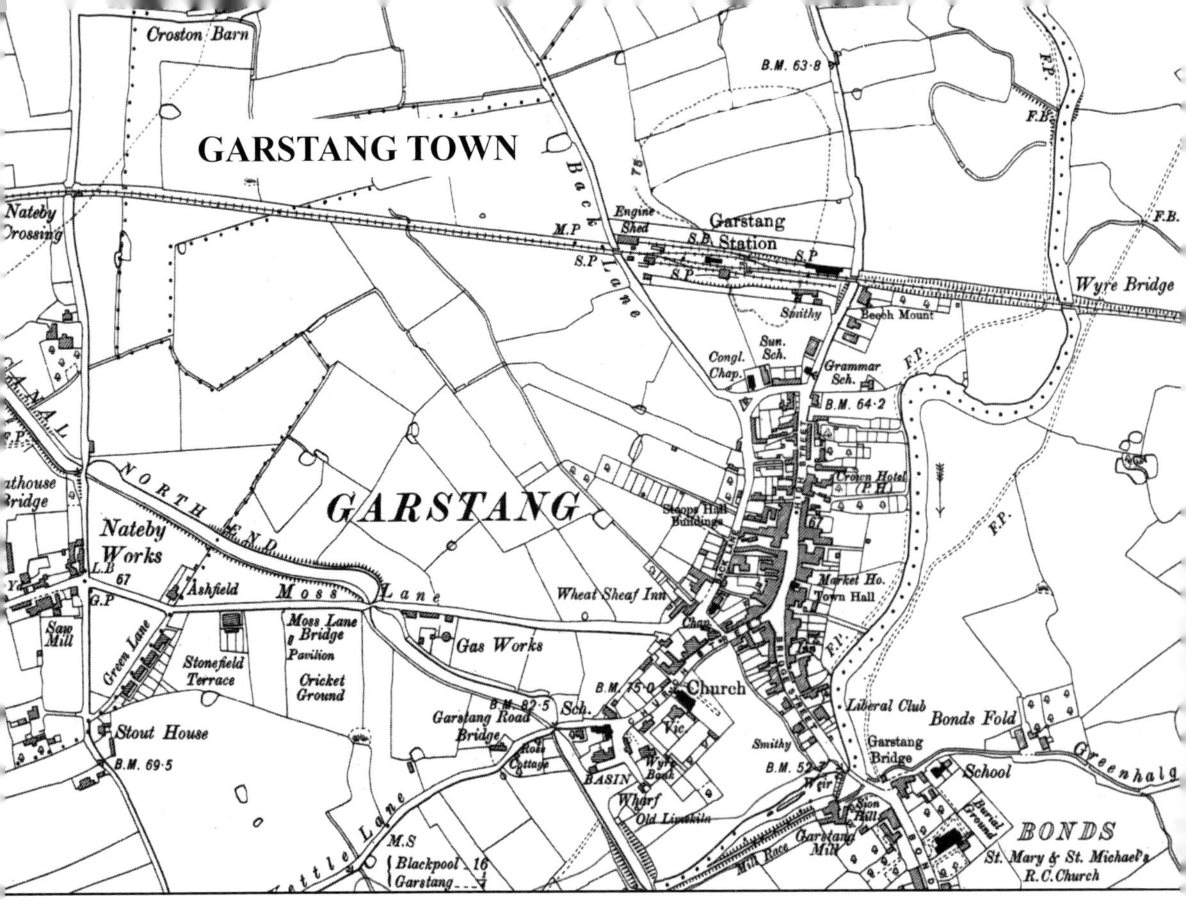

XVII. This 1914 6ins map shows the station layout in better detail. The station opened on 5th December 1870 and boasted goods, engine and carriage sheds. The station was rebuilt in 1909 with an island platform accessed via the footbridge with the station building on the latter together with a signal box, a two-road engine shed to the northwest, and new carriage sheds. The suffix 'Town' was added to the station's name on 2nd July 1924. The station closed to passengers on 31st March 1930 and to goods on 16th August 1965. The site is now occupied by housing development around Station Way.

67. Standing in the original station circa 1874 is Manning Wardle 0-4-0ST *Union* hauling a single composite coach. (Knott End Collection courtesy of RailScot).

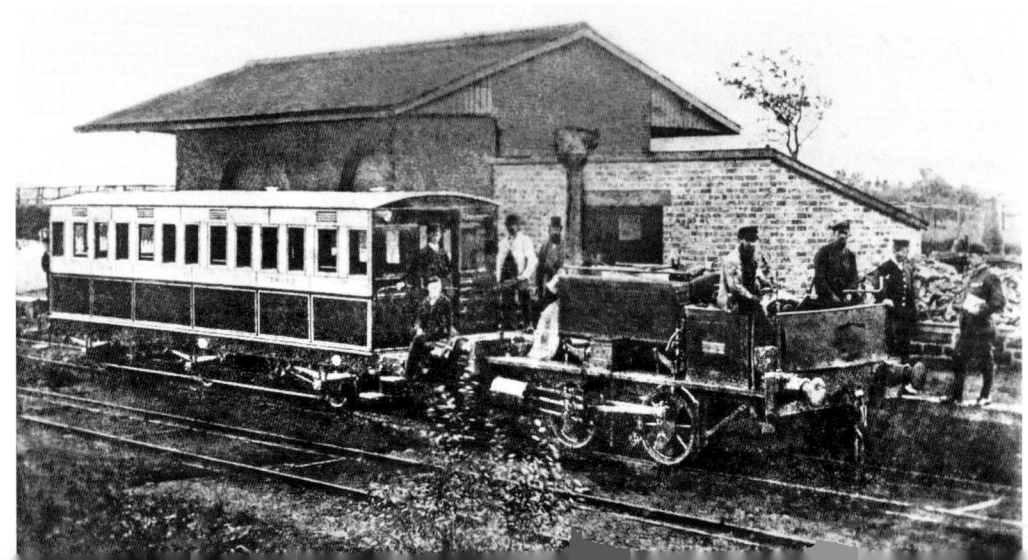

68. In this undated shot Manning Wardle 2-6-0T *Blackpool*, acquired by the railway in 1909, is seen at Garstang Town heading a typical passenger service. (Lens of Sutton Association)

69. The station, as rebuilt in 1908, clearly showing the station building incorporating the signal box located on the island platform, which was accessed by the footbridge. (Lens of Sutton Association)

70. In latter days Black 5s were the mainstay of the line and here no. 45438 is seen shunting in the station yard, most probably in the early 1950s judging by the amount of freight being handled. Ivatt 2MT 2-6-0s would have also been seen on the branch. This shot was taken from the eastern end of the island platform, which affords a view of the former carriage sheds that were void of tracks by then. (Knott End Collection)

71. In this undated photo Black 5 no. 45070 and wagons are seen passing through the station en route to Pilling. The goods shed can be seen on the right and the signal box to the left; the other station buildings were behind the signal box. By then the footbridge at the far end of the platform had been removed. (Knott End Collection)

72. Black 5 no. 45449 waits for the gates at Nateby Lane Crossing to be secured before proceeding towards Nateby in the early 1960s. The crossing keeper's cottage has survived at least until until 2024, although its future is in doubt as a large housing development for the area had been approved. (Knott End Collection)

NATEBY

XVIII. Nateby station was one mile from the village and was somewhat remote. It was first named Winmarleigh after the local landowner at that time, then was renamed after his death in 1902. Originally it was only a halt with the platform on the southern side of the line along with a siding and head shunt. It received a passing loop in 1909 and a second platform on the northern side, and by 1910 it also had a goods siding with cattle dock. According to timetables Nateby was a request stop for much of its life. Passenger services along with freight facilities were withdrawn in 1930 and the line west of Garstang Town along with the station closed altogether in 1963.

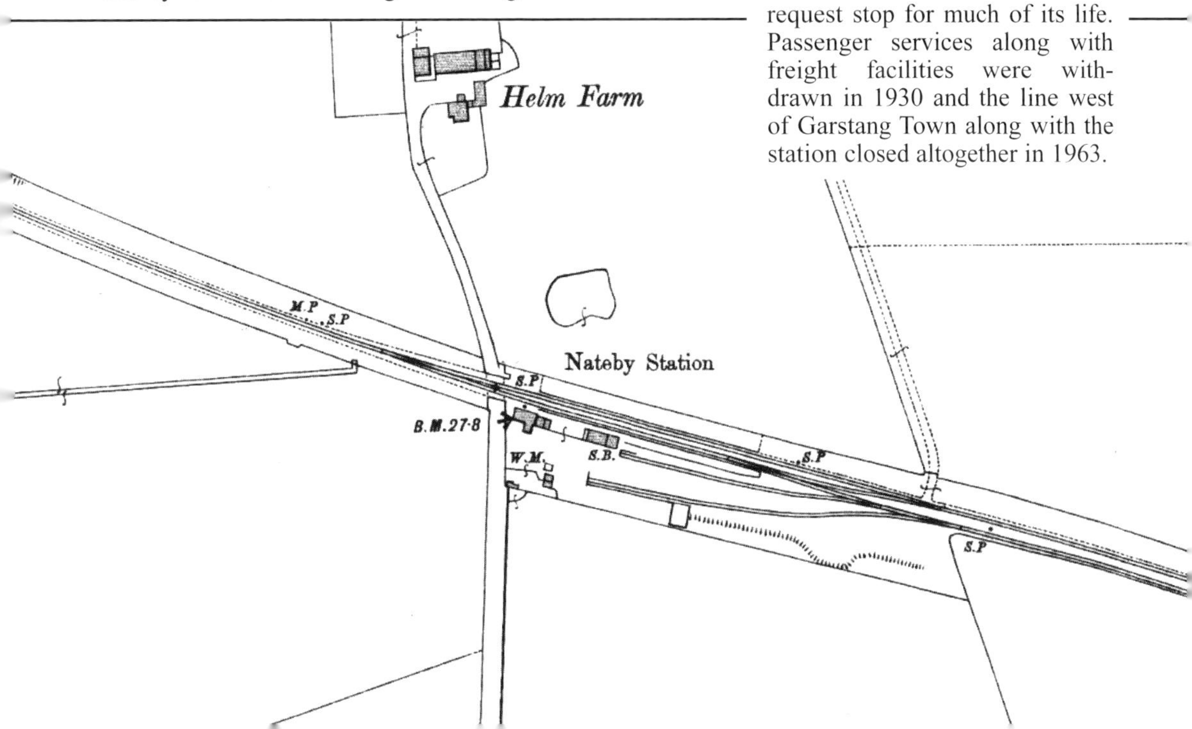

73. The station circa 1909 is sporting the new signal box to the left. Installation of new signalling and construction of a new down platform are nearing completion. A six-wheeled carriage can be seen on the right of the photograph. (Lens of Sutton Association)

74. LNWR Railmotor no. 10698 and railway staff posing at Nateby station on the final day of passenger services on Saturday, 29th March 1930 as there was no Sunday service.
(Knott End Collection)

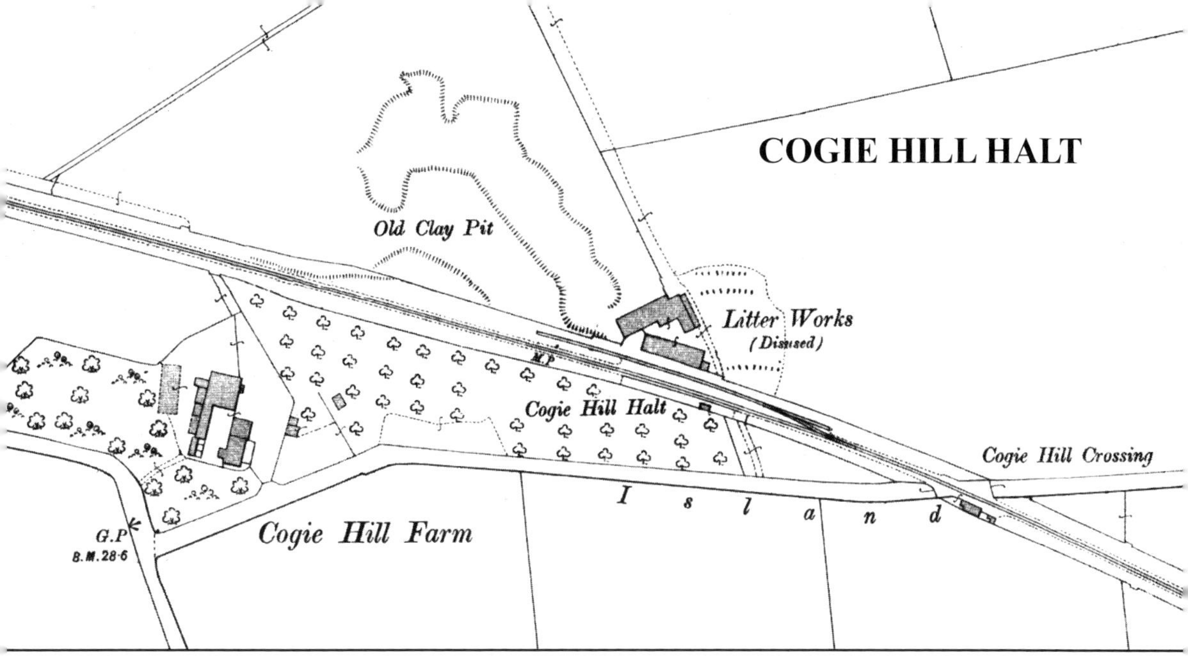

COGIE HILL HALT

XIX. Trains would stop at the level crossing upon request right from the start but there was no platform until after the financial settlement with the Winmarleigh Estate in 1893. Cogie Hill was designated as a stopping place as it was situated on one of the main road routes through the area and was a convenient place to access the railway for the people living nearby. Places like Nateby, Winmarleigh and Cogie Hill were not recognisable villages as such but rather a collection of farms and cottages. The 1915 timetable shows it as a request stop: Thursdays and Fridays going east (Friday was market day in (Garstang) and Fridays and Saturdays only going west. It closed to passengers, like all other stations on the line, on 31st March 1930.

75. An unidentified LMS Black 5 crosses the minor road at Cogie Hill with a goods train returning from Pilling towards Garstang, probably sometime in the early 1960s. There was a small request halt here from the date the line opened until the withdrawal of passenger services in 1930. The crossing keeper's cottage survived the 1963 closure of the line. (Knott End Collection)

Cockerham Cross Halt

A remote station opened on 5th December 1870; an 1892 map indicates that there was no platform, although one published in 1912 does show one. There is no record of when it was constructed; maybe it was an omission by the map makers at the time. Along with Cogie Hill Halt, Cockerham Cross trains only stopped on Thursdays and Saturdays, as required. The suffix 'Halt' was added to the station name in July 1923 and, like all remaining stations, it closed on 31st March 1930.

Garstang Road Halt

The station was opened by the London Midland and Scottish Railway in October 1923 and closed not long after, on 31st March 1930.

PILLING

XX. The station opened on 5th December 1870 to serve the villages of Pilling and Stake Pool (also known locally as Stakepool). It was located close by Stake Pool village and was sometimes called Stake Pool station, although called Pilling it was about 1½ miles (2.4 km) by road from the village. Due to the financial condition of the G&KER the plan to open the line to Knott End failed and the station opened as the terminus of the line from Garstang & Catterall. Seeing the potential of opening the line to the coast, the company was acquired by the Knott End Railway and the line was extended to Knott End on 30th July 1908. With the new found fortunes, a second platform was added with platforms on either side of the passing loop. The goods yard was extended, a goods shed provided and a substantially larger station building was constructed by the southern platform in 1903 before the KER takeover. The station was closed to passenger traffic on 31st March 1930. This extract is dated 1912.

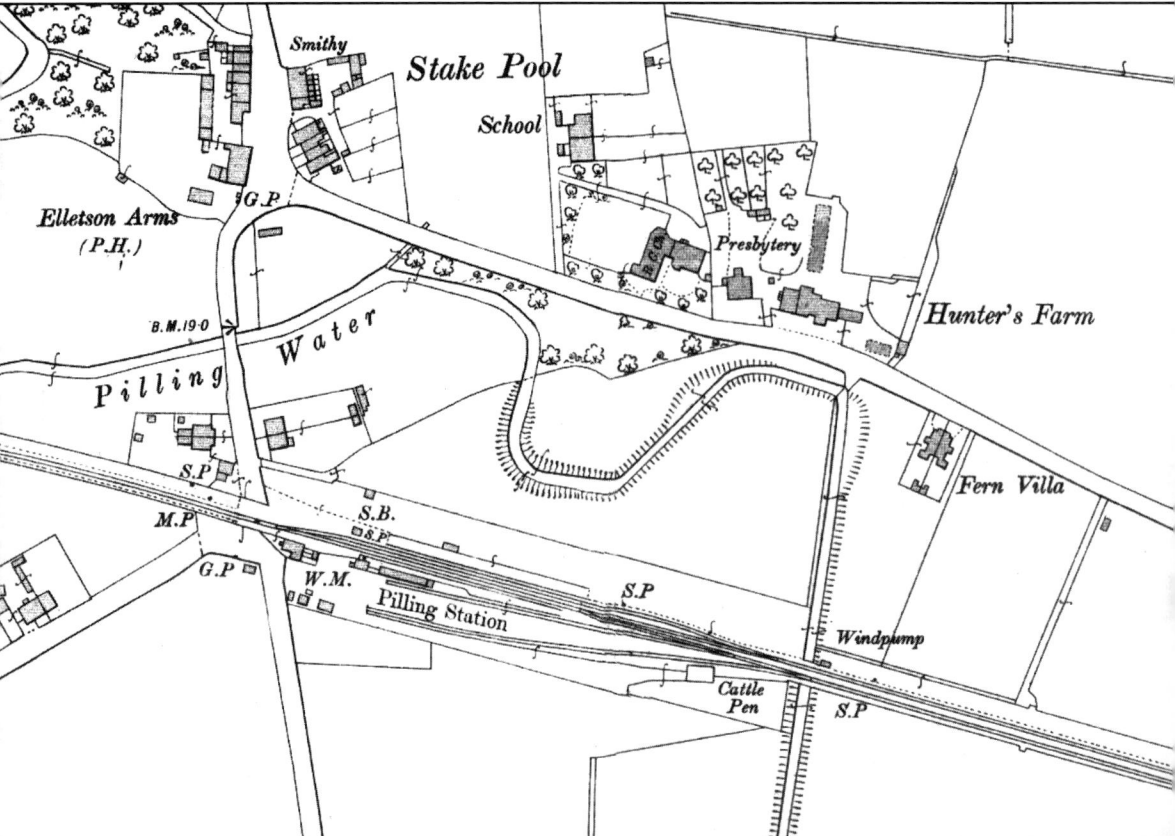

76. A service arriving at Pilling in around 1905 that at the time was the end of the line from Garstang & Catterall. (John Alsop)

77. A station scene circa 1908 showing construction work associated with the second platform and passing loop. 0-6-0ST *Jubilee Queen* is seen in charge of what appears to be an army volunteers special. (Lens of Sutton Association)

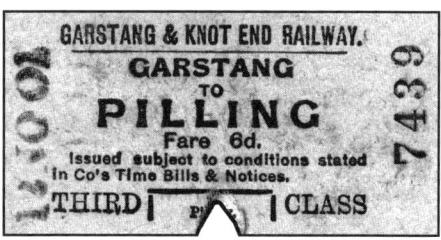

78. A rail tour to Pilling on 1st May 1954, which was organised by the Manchester and Stephenson Locomotive Societies. Passenger accommodation comprised former MR, LMS and LNWR coaches hauled by ex-LMS Fowler 2-6-4T no. 42316. By then the line beyond Pilling was closed and the station loop had been disconnected that required dividing the train and a number of shunting moves to run the engine round. (Knott End Collection)

79. In December 1875 the G&KER acquired Hudswell Clarke 0-6-0ST *Farmer's Friend*. It became known locally as the *Pilling Pig* on account of the squeal made by its whistle that sounded supposedly like a pig being slaughtered. The pictured Hudswell Clarke 0-6-0ST works no. 1885 is displayed at the entrance to the caravan site built on the Knott End line trackbed at Pilling and resembled some of the later locos used on the branch. It was named *Pilling Pig*, an unofficial name for all trains on the railway after *Farmer's Friend*. Note the *Pilling Piglet* in the background. The locomotive posing as the *Pilling Pig* was built in 1955 for the National Coal Board and operated in collieries in Wales until it was taken out of service in 1977. After several years in storage, it was later acquired by the National Museum of Wales that sent it to the Gwili Railway in 1981. With mechanical problems it was cosmetically restored and in 2001 it was moved to Fold House Caravan Park. It is presented in G&KER livery and the number on the cab side '11302' was actually carried by Manning Wardle 0-6-0ST *Knot End*, built in 1908 and scrapped by the LMS in 1924. (Mark Bartlett)

Carr Lane Halt

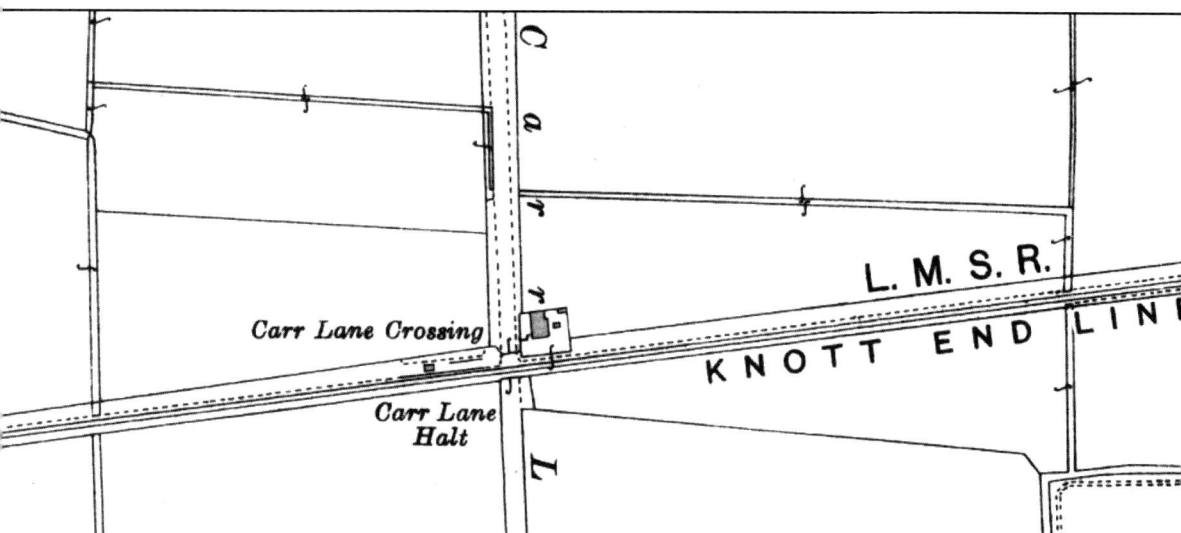

XXI. The station was opened by the Knott End Railway in July 1921 and was named after the road where it was located. The station had a short platform, which was later extended and a timber waiting room added as seen in this 1932 map. It became a request stop in the 1921-22 winter timetable and closed on 31st March 1930. There were no goods facilities at Carr Lane station.

PREESALL

XXII. The station was opened by the Knott End Railway on 3rd August 1908. It was situated on the east side of Park Lane. To the south was the goods yard that had a goods shed, loading ramp, crane and weighbridge. The station was closed to passengers on 31st March 1930 and goods on 13th November 1950. The platform face remains in place to this day. The map is dated 1912.

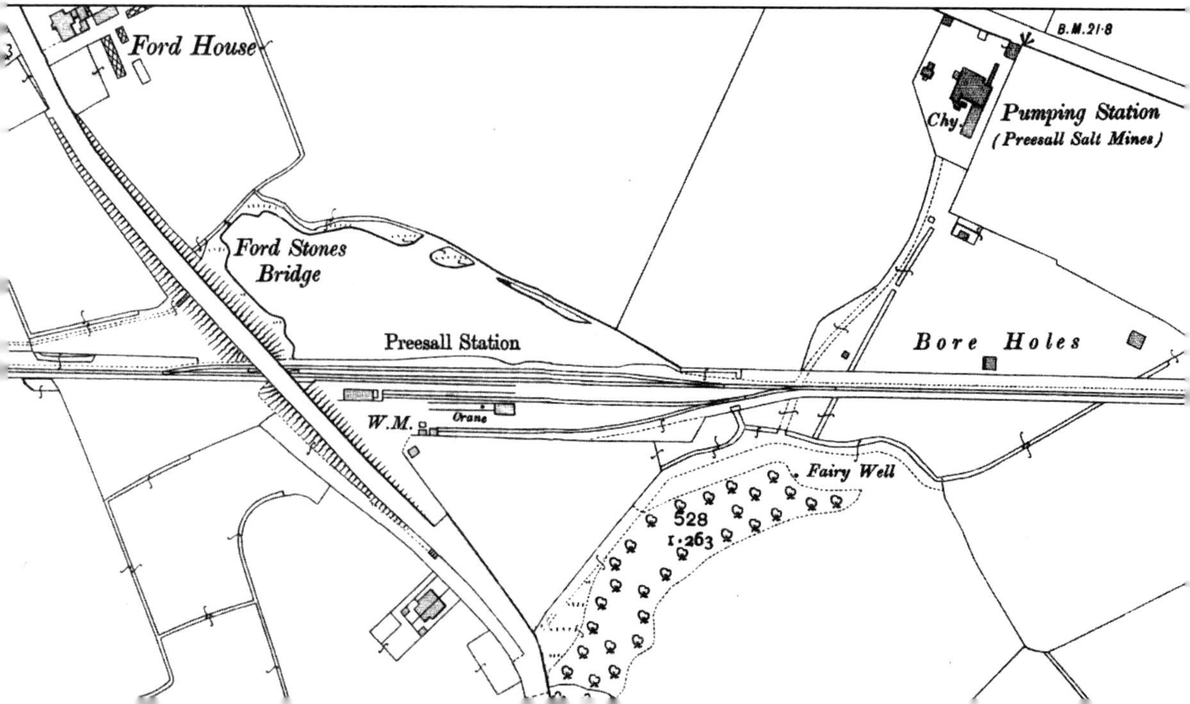

80. Notable in this 1908 shot is the over bridge. The KER had originally planned a level crossing at this point in line with other road crossings on the line but the authorities insisted on this expensive bridge, which added considerably to the construction costs. The embankments still stand today but the bridge has been removed and the gap infilled. (Robert Humm coll.)

81. An interesting image of the brand new and almost finished Preesall station on the 1908 extension of the line from Pilling to Knott End. Manning Wardle 0-6-0T *Knott End* is seen pulling in with two veranda composite coaches and a guards van. This shot was taken from the road bridge at the western end of the station. The station was only open for 22 years and, after closure to passengers in March 1930, goods trains continued to pass through until 1950.
(Lens of Sutton Association)

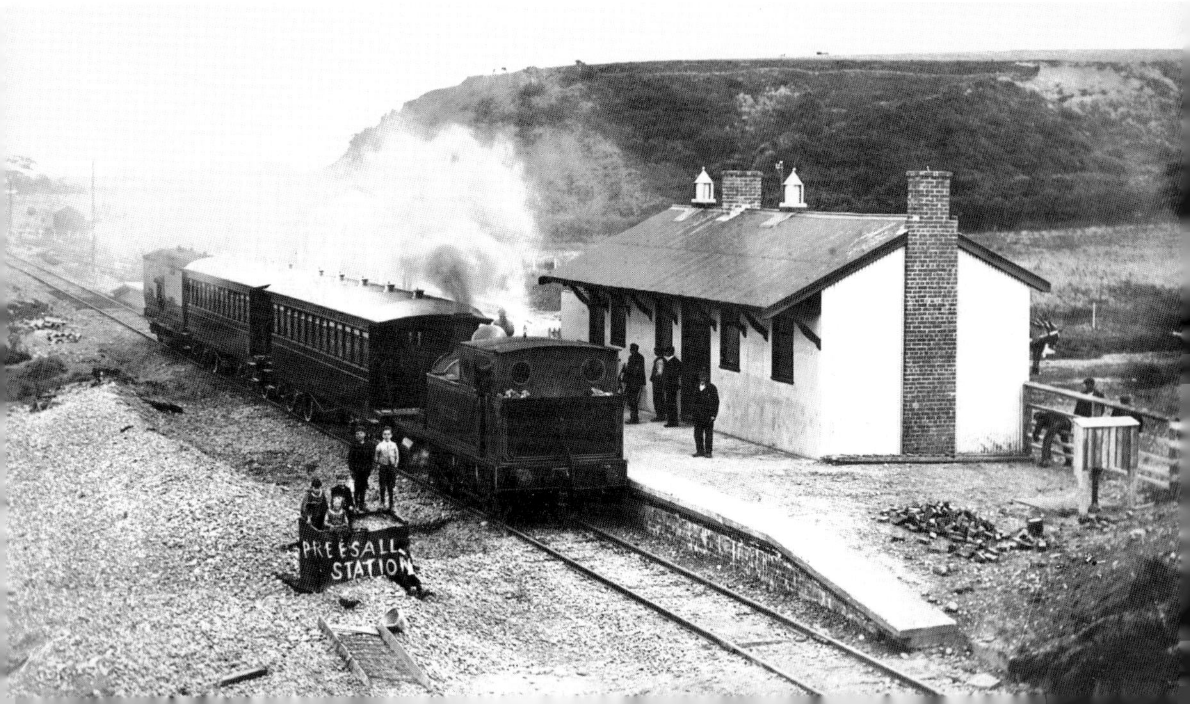

82. This 1908 shot shows construction workers laying the final section of the KER line approaching the Hackensall Crossing on the outskirts of Knott End. (John Alsop)

KNOTT END

83. The station frontage as seen on 16th July 1965. The building then housed a cafe and ironically it was used as a bus waiting room. Since that photo was taken, the former station has been doubled in height and extensively modernised but is still home to a cafe.
(J.Marshall/Kidderminster Railway Museum)

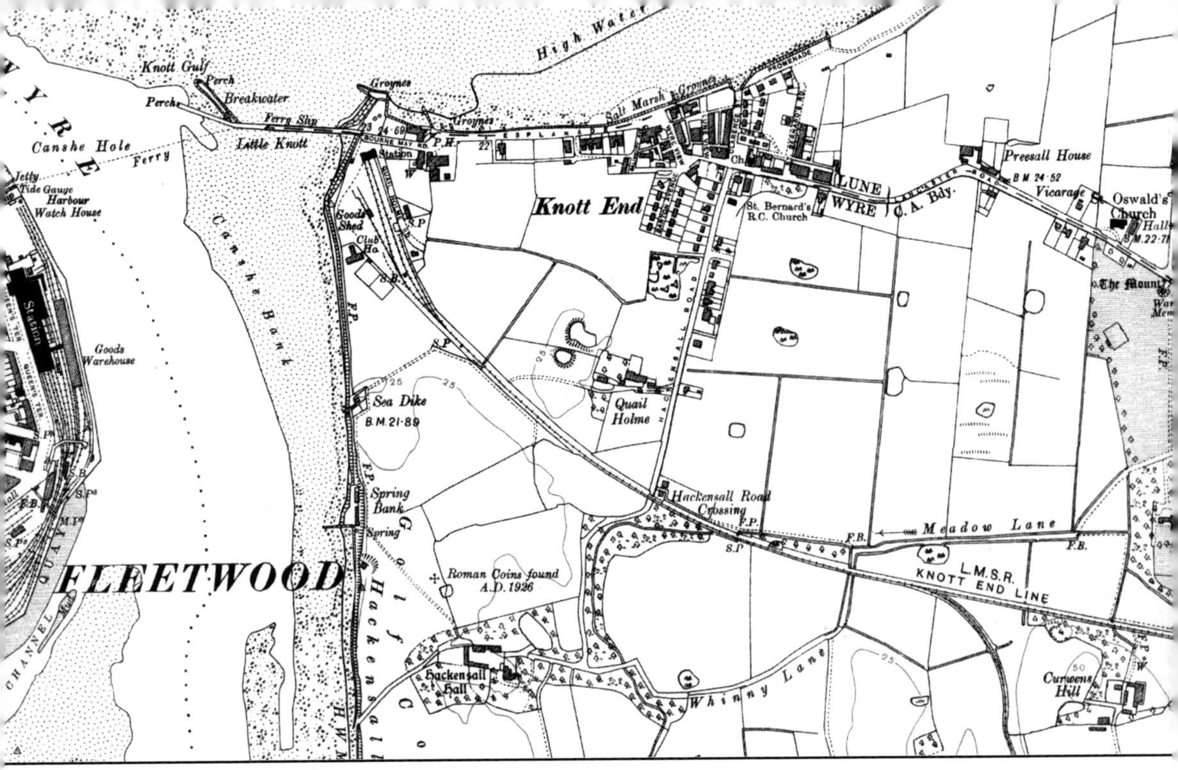

XXIII. The station served Knott End on Sea and boasted a ferry service to Fleetwood that contributed to the railway's fortunes. The station was opened by the KER on 30th July 1908; it closed to passengers on 31st March 1930 and to goods on 13th November 1950. Apart from regular passenger and freight traffic, the line benefitted from: [1] significant tourism due, to a large extent, to the Fleetwood ferry; [2] the territorial army that trained nearby, largely between 1906 and 1909, and [3] to a greater extent traffic generated by the Perusall salt industry. In 1934 four possibly five camping coaches were located at Knott End and referred to as caravans by the LMS. These were located in the warehouse siding some 50 yards from the station buildings. After the line to Knott End closed to passengers, holidaymakers, if not travelling by road, would make their way by rail to Fleetwood and then the ferry across the Wyre estuary. The caravans were last used in 1939 and subsequently removed. This 6ins map is dated 1933.

Bradshaw, July 1924

Miles	GARSTANG AND CATTERALL and KNOTT END.—(3rd class only).—L. M. & S. (late Knott End).									Miles										
		Week Days only.										Week Days only.								
		mrn	mrn	mrn	aft 1&3	aft A	aft	aft	aft 1&3	aft			mrn	mrn	mrn 1&3	mrn A	aft	aft	aft	aft	aft
	Garstang and Catterall..dep.	....	8 25	10 38	1 25	....	5 5	4 27	5 8	8 50	....	Knott End......dep.	....	8 5	9 25	....	12 30	2 30	4 0	6 18	7 55	....
1¼	Garstang Town......	7 15	8 35	10 48	....	1 35	....	5 15	5 50	7 13	8 56	....	1½	Preesall.........	....	8 9	9 30	....	12 35	2 35	4 5	6 23	8 0	....
3¾	Nateby.........	7 19	8 41	10 53	....	1 40	....	5 20	5 55	7 18	....	....	4	Carr Lane Halt......	....	8 15	9 37	....	12 32	2 42	4 12	6 30	8 8	....
5	Cogie Hill Halt	....	8 45	10 57	....	1 44	....	5 24	....	7 22	....	....	4½	Pilling.........	....	8 18	9 41	....	12 36	2 46	4 16	6 34	8 11	....
5¾	Cockerham Cross Halt	....	8 49	11 1	....	1 48	....	5 28	....	7 26	....	....	5	Garstang Road Halt...	....	....	9 44	....	12 39	....	4 19	6 37	8 15	....
6¾	Garstang Road Halt...	....	8 49	11 1	....	1 48	....	5 28	....	7 26	....	....	5¾	Cockerham Cross Halt.	....	....	9 46	....	12 41	....	4 21	6 39	8 17	....
7	Pilling.........	7 30	8 53	11 5	....	1 52	....	5 0	3 26	6 7	7 30	....	6¾	Cogie Hill Halt......	....	....	9 49	....	12 44	....	4 23	6 41	8 19	....
7½	Carr Lane Halt	7 32	8 56	11 8	....	1 55	2 52	5 3	5 6	8 7	7 33	....	7½	Nateby.........	....	8 26	9 52	....	12 47	....	4 27	6 45	8 23	....
10	Preesall......	7 40	9 4	11 16	....	2 3	3 0	5 43	6 1	9 7	7 41	....	9½	Garstang Tn.(328, 334	7 40	8 10	8 33	10 2	12 57	....	4 37	6 55	8 27	....
11¼	Knott End......arr.	7 45	9 10	11 22	....	2 9	3 6	5 49	6 2	17	7 47	....	11¼	Garstg & Catterall arr	7 46	8 16	8 40	10 10	1 5	....	4 45	7 3	8 35	....

A Fridays only

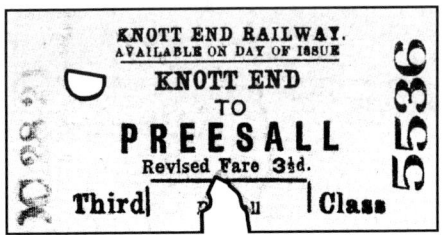 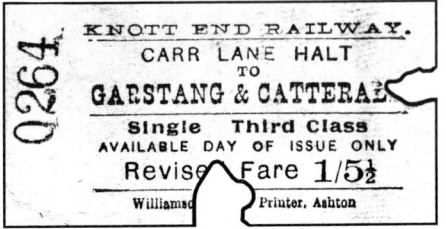

84. Judging by the pristine condition of the platforms, locomotive and carriages, this image of a train leaving Knott End station was probably taken around the time of its opening in 1908 as evidenced by the ongoing construction and tidying up works. The locomotive is Manning Wardle 0-6-0T *Knott End* built for the opening of the extension of the line from Pilling. The open veranda carriages, built by the Birmingham Carriage & Wagon Company of Smedwick, were later used on the Wanlockhead branch in Scotland after the branch went over to using railmotors hired by the KER from the LNWR. (Lens of Sutton Association)

85. Shortly after acquiring the G&KER in 1908 the KER sent *Jubilee Queen* and *New Century* for servicing and were replaced temporarily by two LNWR 0-6-0STs nos. 1325 and 3210. In this picture no. 1325 and the crew are posing for the camera at Knott End. (Anthony Coppin collection)

86. Volunteers detraining their horses having arrived at a rather busy station and sidings on 27th June 1909. (John Alsop)

87. Taken on 14th March 1931 almost a year after passenger services were withdrawn, as evidenced by the grass on the platform, ex-LNWR Webb 'Cauliflower' class 2F no. 8525, later 28525, is ready to depart with a typical mixed freight. (Robert Humm coll.)

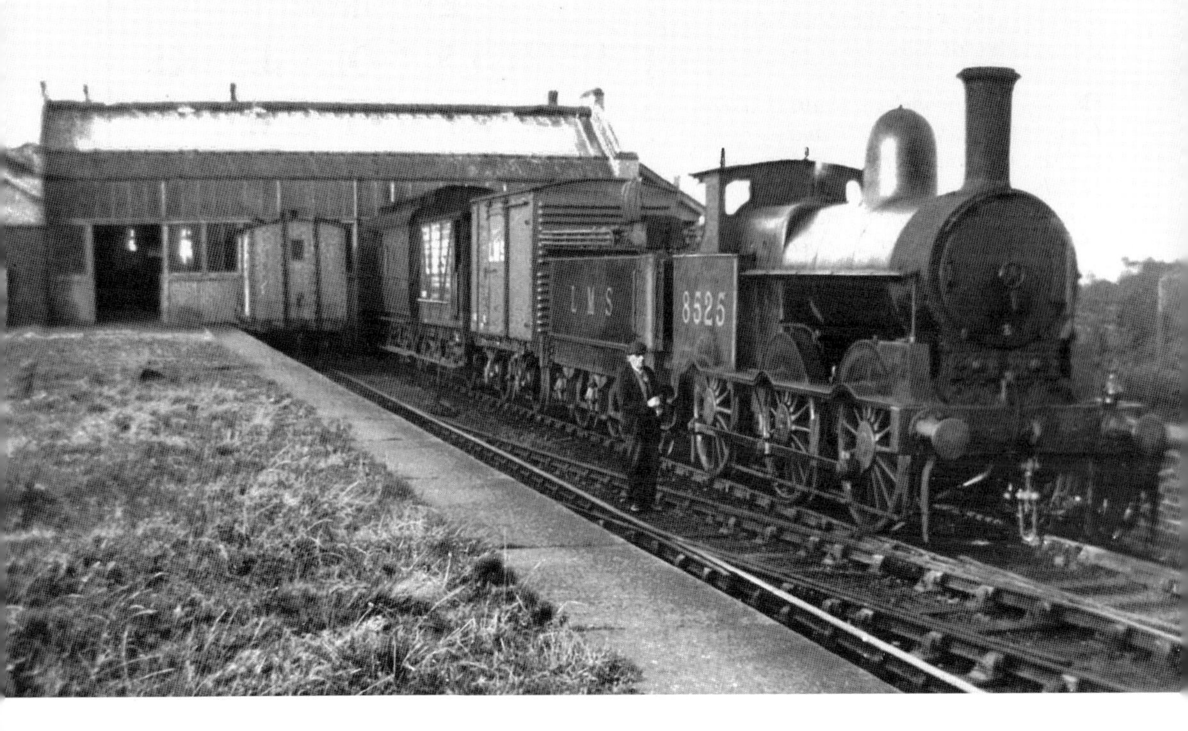

88. The former goods shed and station were photographed long after the camping coaches had been removed; the track was either overgrown or lifted at this point. The shed was then home to the Jogo Syphon Cistern Company and the car parked nearby looks very much like an Austin A125 Sheerline Estate. (Robert Humm coll.)

→ The Fleetwood and Knott End Golf Club was founded in 1910 and no doubt the railway and ferry from Fleetwood and the direct line to Knott End played a part in its development and patronage. 'Fleetwood' was later dropped from the club's name. It is a links course more or less bounded by the route of the former mineral railway - see map XXIV on the following page. (Robert Humm coll.)

KNOTT END RAILWAY.

Excellent
18-HOLE GOLF LINKS
at KNOTT END.

Cheap Day, Week-end, and long date bookings, now in force to KNOTT END, *via* Garstang & Catterall Junction from Manchester, Liverpool, Bolton, Wigan, Blackburn, Oldham, &c., &c.

For particulars see special bills or apply at the Booking Office.

G. ERROLL WORTHINGTON,
General Manager.

Mineral Railway

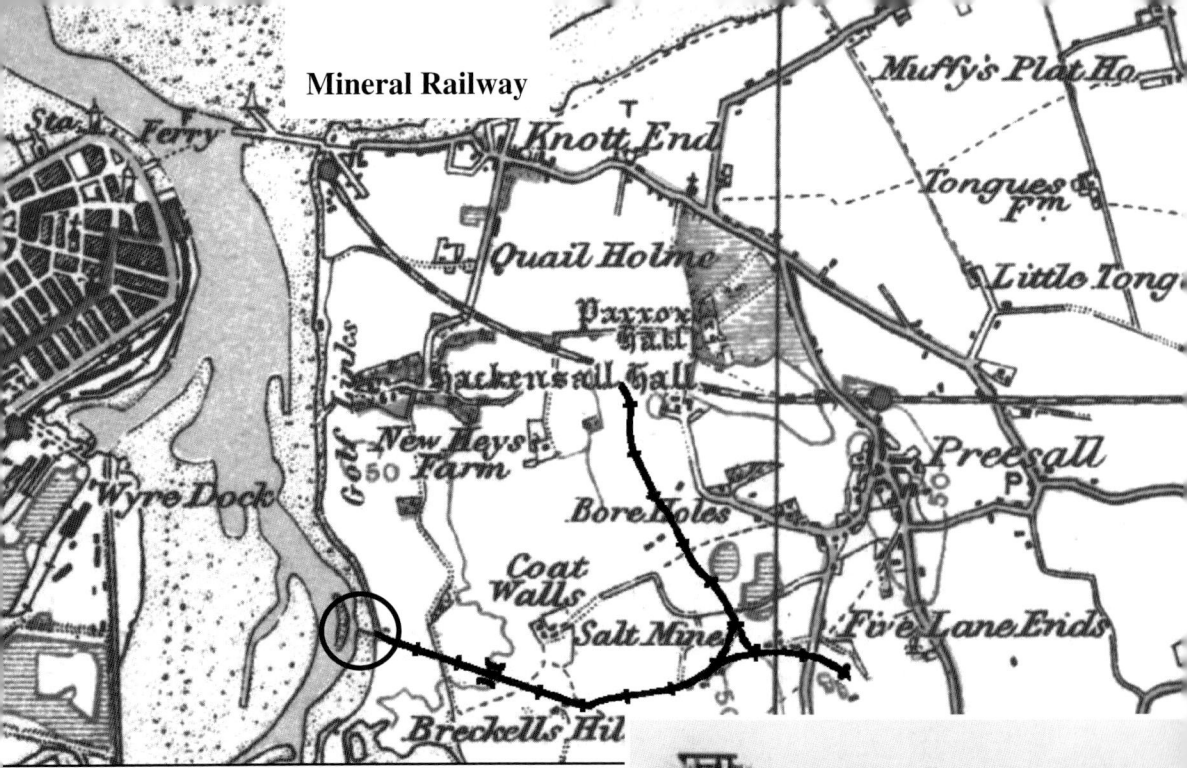

XXIV. This 1933 (1in to 1 mile) map shows the standard gauge mineral railway, which has been darkened to better show its location. It branched off the main line southeast of Knott End station and turned south to the United Alkali Company, formerly the Fleetwood Salt Company, salt mines and processing plant; it then headed due west to the jetty on the River Wyre. Initially the mineral railway, constructed in 1893, connected the mines and works with the jetty but the United Alkali Company was keen to have access to the mainline for both carrying rock salt and receiving coal for its boilers. In this regard it had been in talks with the G&KER without much success, but, when the act was passed on 12th August 1898 authorising the new operator, the KER, to extend the railway beyond Pilling, it contained

Inset: The United Alkali Company rail-served jetty on the River Wyre is circled on the map. The company's locomotives hauled hoppers on to the jetty where the salt would be loaded on to ships via the tipping equipment. (Anthony Coppin coll.)

provision for a connection with the company's internal system. This however proved difficult as the KER resources were stretched and insolvency loomed and so further use had to be made of the jetty. With the extension to Knott End complete, the KER was keen to get its hands on the rock salt traffic to Widnes and St Helens and deliver coal to the plant. During 1911 and 1912 the extension northwards was constructed to the mainline as shown on the map, together with a loop, and by 1913 the KER started to benefit from the traffic. The United Alkali Company had its own locomotives for internal operations through the years: Manning Wardle's 0-4-0ST *Union* ex-G&KER, 0-6-0ST *Ajax* of 1864 and another Manning Wardle engine *Sir Max* of 1874. Transferring goods to/from the railway varied; on occasion wagons were left at Knott End to be collected and, on others, the KER would drop off/collect wagons from the company sidings. Salt traffic continued to increase thereafter and throughout WWI, as shipping was severely disrupted, reaching its zenith in 1920 with a corresponding increase in coal deliveries but by 1922 rail carriage of rock salt had fallen significantly as traffic reverted to cheaper shipments by sea. This practice was continued by the company's successor, Imperial Chemical Industries. The fall in salt traffic came about around 1920 when changes in the processes carried out at Widnes meant that significantly less rock salt from Preesall was required. Carriage of salt by rail continued thereafter until mining ceased altogether in 1931. There is no clear indication when the mineral railway was taken out of use but when the former KER line was closed in 1950 the points to the railway were extant but the tracks beyond had been lifted. The only significant trace of the railway today is the Knott End Golf Club-owned jetty, which is in a state of disrepair.

6. Lancaster Old Goods Line

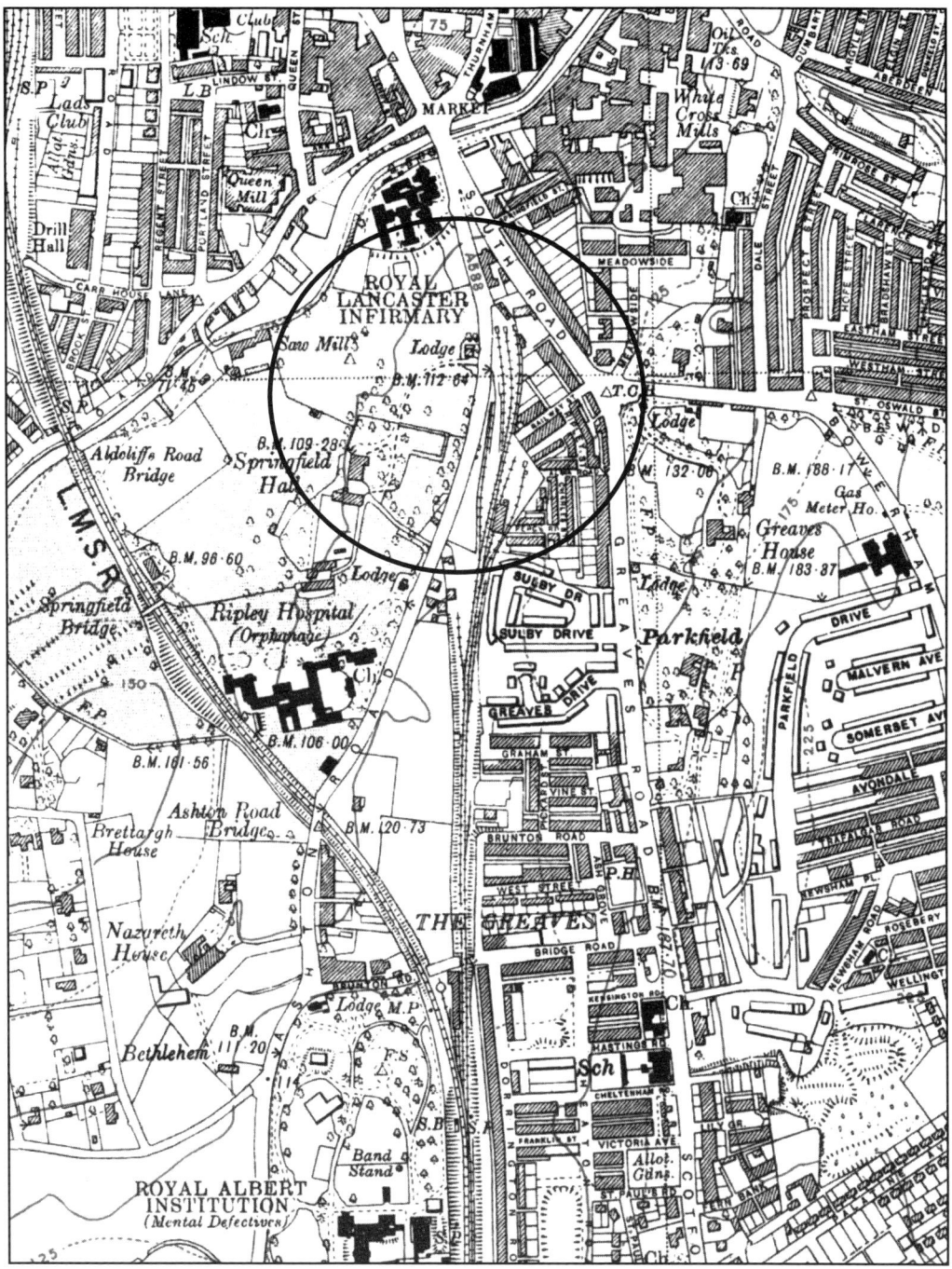

XXV. This 1946 6ins map shows the route of the Lancaster & Preston Junction railway line from Lancaster Old Junction running north to the freight yard (circled); the line was lifted beyond this point where it would have run into the former terminus, which is the building now occupied by the NHS, situated at the junction of South and Ashton Roads, near the top of the map just before the Royal Lancaster Infirmary. Access to the branch was controlled by Lancaster No. 1 signal box.

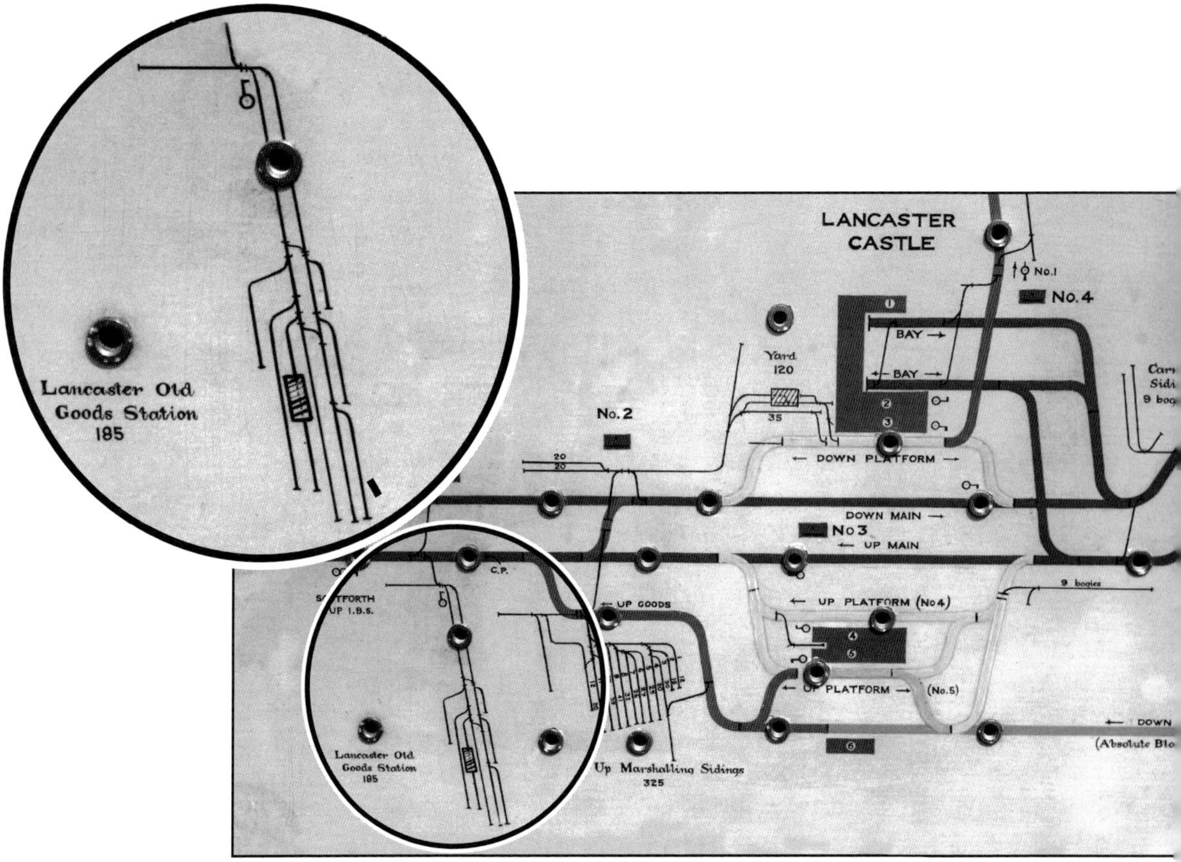

XXVI. This image shows part of the Carnforth section controllers train board then at Preston station, which shows the line (bottom left) as it was in 1958. The 'branch' was shown as Lancaster Old Goods Line and the suffix '185' shows the number of wagons that could be stabled there. (Ron Herbert)

89. On 26th October 1967 ex-LNER Gresley 4-6-2 no. 4472 *Flying Scotsman* is seen heading north with the RCTS Moorlander tour. In the distance is Lancaster no. 1 signal box and straight ahead Ripley loco shed; at that point the mainline curves away to the left between the two structures before descending into Lancaster. (Peter van Campenhout)

90. The aforementioned Ripley shed, also known as 'Bridge Road' and affectionately as the 'Dog Kennel', is seen here on 6th April 1950 having closed in 1934 along with the turntable. Note the water tank on top of the shed. (Cumbria Railways Association/Pearsall Collection)

91. On 23rd May 1964 BR Standard Clan class 6MT 4-6-2 no. 72007 *Clan MacKintosh* is seen at the head of 1Z12 RCTS 'Ribble - Lune Railtour' having reversed down the branch towards the coal yard. The houses in the background are on Railway Street. (Peter van Campenhout)

92. BR Ivatt class 4 2-6-0 Mogul no. 43106 is seen stabled on the Old line on 12th February 1967 heading a ballast working in connection with the electrification of the West Coast Main Line. At the front of the engine, the steeple of Ripley St Thomas School can just be seen through the trees. These class 4 locomotives were affectionately know as 'Doodlebugs' or 'Flying Pigs'. No. 43106 was withdrawn on 22nd June 1968 and, in the following August, was acquired from Lostock Hall MPD by the Severn Valley Railway, where it remains in preservation to this day. (Peter van Campenhout)

93. In this undated photo 16T mineral wagons make coal deliveries to the truncated end of the former L&PJR. One of the recipients could well have been coal merchant, W. J. Turner. The line closed for freight on 14th August 1967 and the tracks were taken up not long after. This area now forms part of the Royal Lancaster Infirmary car park on Ashton Road, where remains of the goods platforms can still be seen. (Graham Hibbert/Michael Bolton coll.)

7. Glasson Dock Branch
LANCASTER

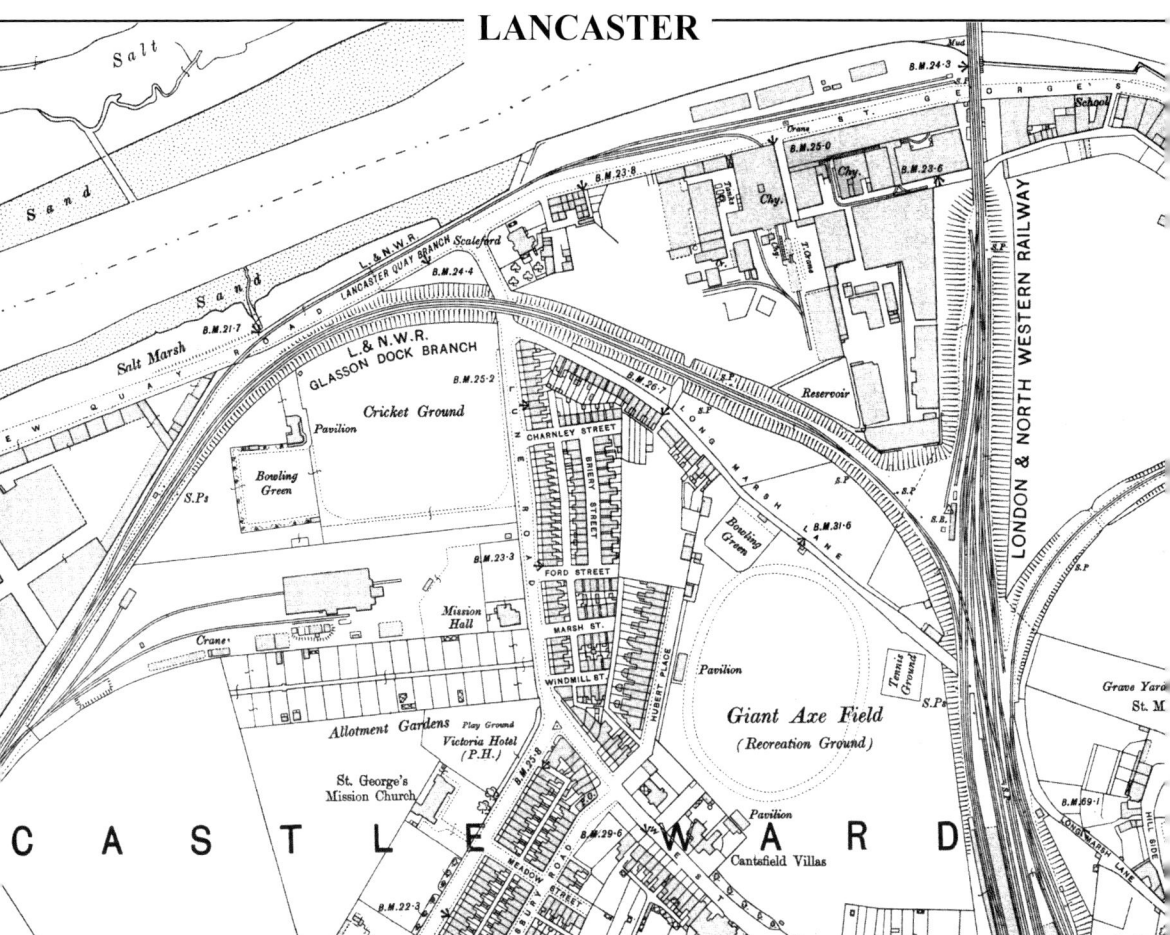

XXVII. The branch diverged to the west just north of Lancaster Castle station, as can be seen in this 1913 map, and fairly rapidly dropped down to more or less sea level. The gradient was such that heavier goods traffic required banking assistance on occasion. After leaving Lancaster station the line was doubled allowing traffic for the quay and the LNWR engineer's yard to work independently of the branch, particularly as any traffic for the quay would need to reverse into either facility. After closure of the Glasson Dock branch the line extended to Freeman's Wood to allow a head shunt for traffic to the quay and engineer's depot. Passenger services to Glasson Dock would have used either platforms 1 or 2 at Lancaster Castle station. Today when travelling north out of Lancaster station some of the earthworks of the branch can still be seen diverging away from the WCML.

LANCASTER and GLASSON DOCK.—L. M. & S.

Miles.	Down.	Week Days only.									Miles.	Up.	Week Days only.							
		mrn	mrn	mrn	aft	aft	aft	aft	aft	aft			mrn	mrn	aft	aft	aft	aft	aft	aft
		d	S	d	E	d	S	x	d	d	S	x				d	x	d	d	S	x
	Lancaster (C.) dep.	7 0	9 10	1155	1210	1240	2 15	5 0	6 10	7 30	9 0		Glasson Dock ..... dep.	8 25	1010	1 25	3 5	5 25	6 45	8 0	9 30
4	Conder Green	a	a	a	a	a	a	a	a	a	a	1	Conder Green.....	[6 19	b	b	b	b	b	b	b
5	Glasson Dock. arr.	7 15	9 25	1210	1225	1255	2 30	5 15	6 25	7 45	9 15	5	Lancaster †† 328, arr.	8 40	1022	1 40	3 20	5 40	7 0	8 15	9 45

a Stop to set down.   **b** Stop to take up only.   **d** One class only   **E** Except Saturdays.   **S** Saturdays only.
X Wednesdays and Saturdays.   †† Castle; about ¼ mile to Green Ayre Station.

Bradshaw, July 1924

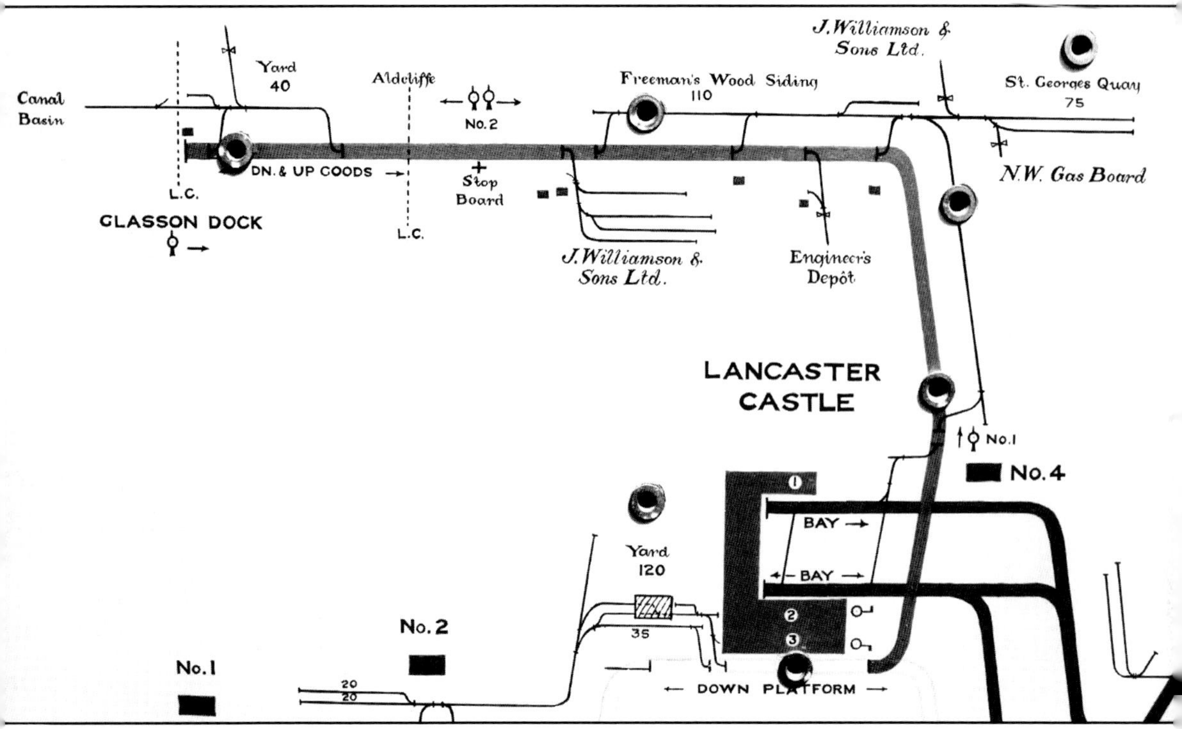

XXVIII. Another image that shows part of the Carnforth section controllers train board at Preston station covering the Glasson Dock branch. The bold line leads off the WCML through platform 3 that would be the route for freight traffic, while passenger services would start/finish in either platform 1 or 2 at Lancaster Castle. (Ron Herbert)

94. The RCTS Glasson Dock brake van tour returning from Glasson Dock on 20th June 1964 is hauled by Ivatt 2-6-0 no. 46433. This was the final tour on the branch and the section from Freeman's Wood to Glasson Dock was taken out of use some three months later. (Ron Herbert)

ASHTON HALL HALT

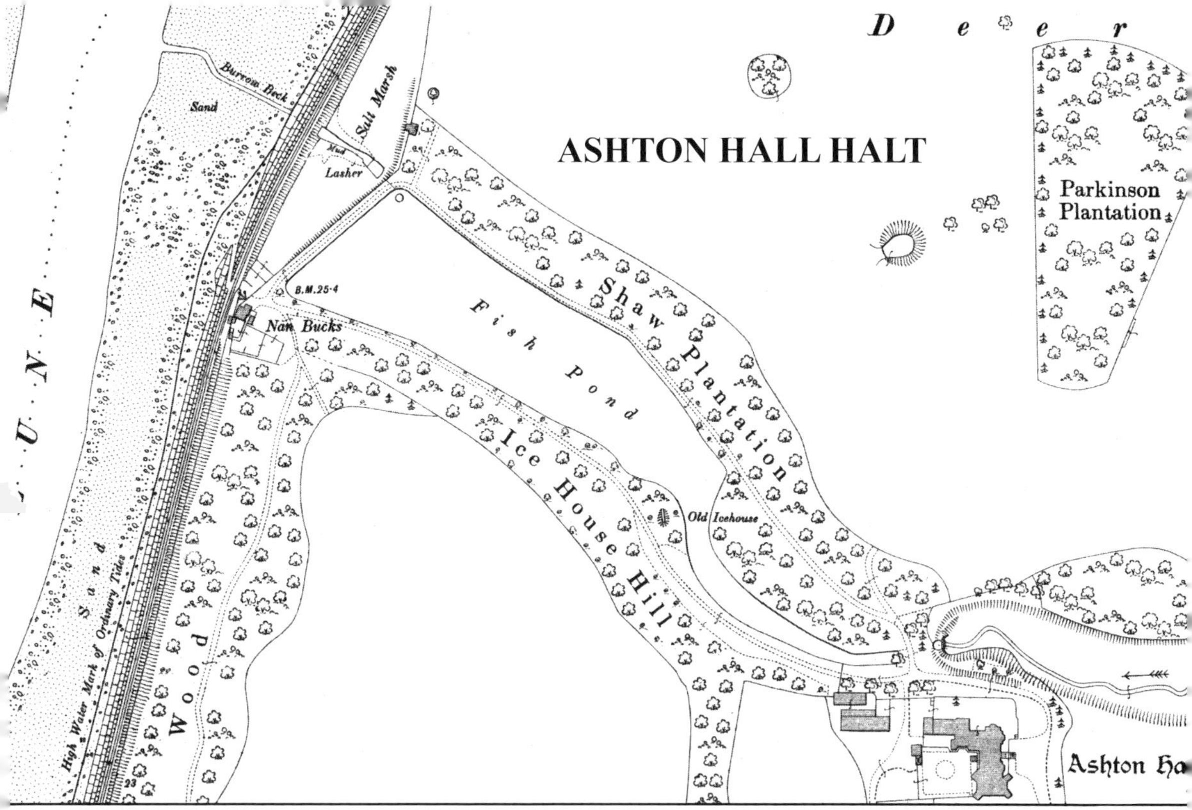

XXIX. Ashton Hall Halt is located next to Nan Bucks. Ashton Hall railway station was a private halt and request stop serving Ashton Hall, the home of Lord Ashton. It opened after August 1883 as Ashton Hall and later the suffix 'Halt' was added; the station closed on 7th July 1930. The station building and platform still stand and Ashton Hall is now the Lancaster Golf Clubhouse. The trackbed through the station is now part of the Lancashire Coastal Way.

95. Long-disused Ashton Hall Halt looking southwest; the photograph was probably taken in the 1960s when as-needed freight services continued on the branch. The building and platform are still in place although the latter is heavily overgrown. (Graham Hibbert/Michael Bolton coll.)

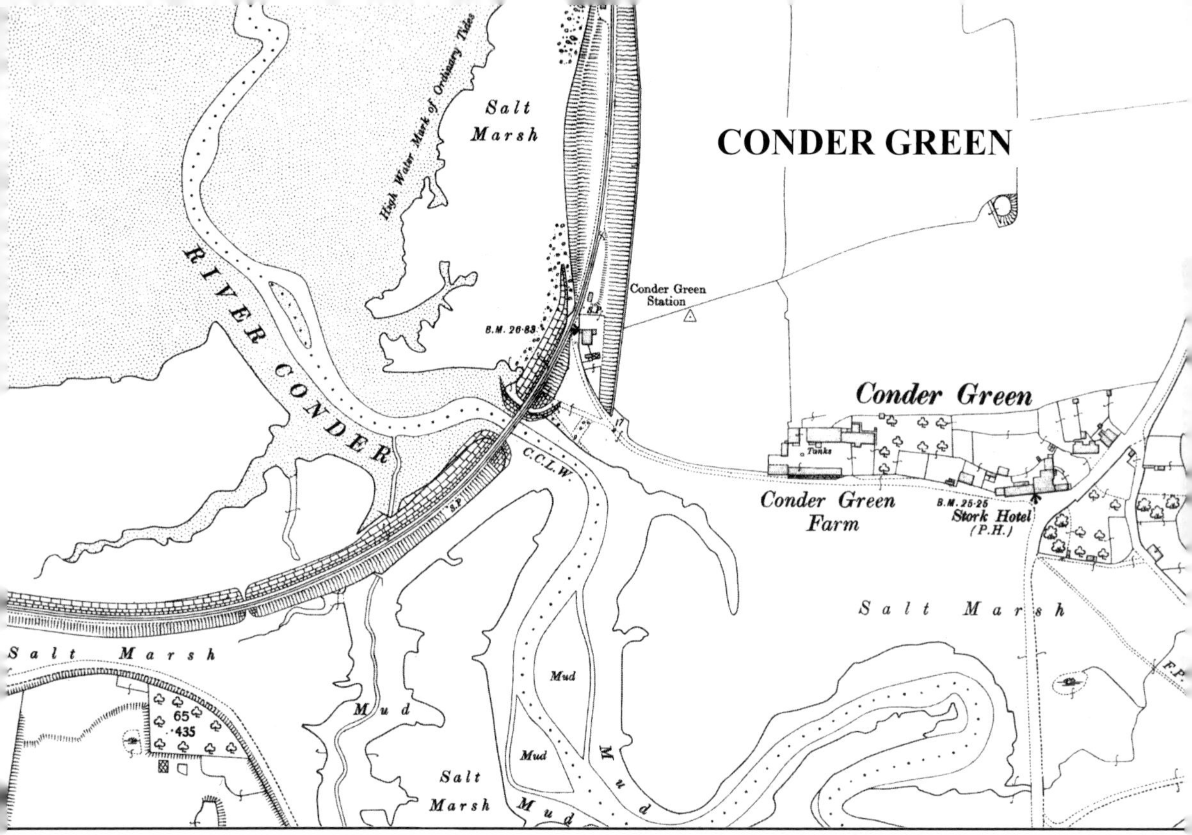

CONDER GREEN

XXX. Situated less than a mile from Glasson Dock, Conder Green station served the nearby hamlet. It opened on 5th November 1883 and closed on 7th July 1930. The station building still stands and the trackbed is now part of the Lancashire Coastal Way and the larger Bay Cycleway.

96. Looking north towards Lancaster circa 1948. The station, by then closed, was situated beyond the viaduct taking the line over the River Conder. (Cumbria Railways Association/Rev. Jackson coll.)

97. An unidentified ex-LMS Fowler 4F 0-6-0 crossing the viaduct over the River Conder around 1952. (Cumbria Railways Association/Rev. Jackson coll.)

GLASSON DOCK

XXXI. Glasson Dock station and small goods yard - seen bottom right on this 1913 map - are some distance from the village at the point where the harbour line forks to pass each side of the quay. As with the other two stations on the branch, Glasson Dock was opened for passengers by the LNWR on 9th July 1883 and closed by the LMS on 7th July 1930. Like the other sections of the branch, the trackbed through the former station is now part of the Lancashire Coastal Way and Bay Cycleway. The station itself was demolished after goods services ended in 1964.

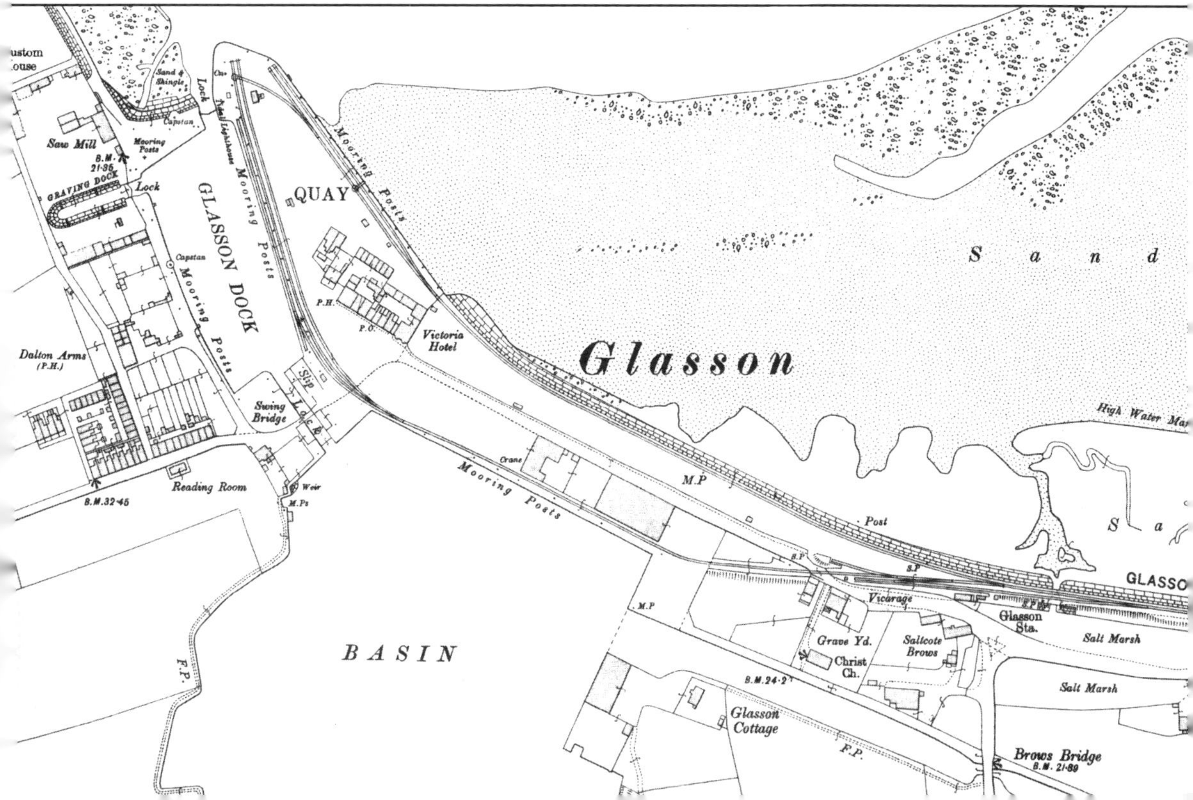

98. An early view of the station looking west towards the warehouses on the quay. (Robert Humm collection)

99. A view looking east towards Conder Green and one of the few shots of a passenger service on the branch. (Cumbria Railways Association)

100. Condemned ex-LMS Fowler class 4P 2-6-4T no. 42301 was withdrawn from Carlisle Kingmoor MPD 19th October 1963. It was moved dead by freight train from Carlisle to Carnforth and then tripped to Lancaster Castle yard for transfer to the ship breakers at Glasson Dock. It was included in 'a run as needed' goods service to Glasson Dock being hauled by Ivatt no. 46422 on 11th March 1964. At Glasson station the Ivatt ran around its train in order to shunt the condemned locomotive into the shipbreaker's yard at the dock. (Ron Herbert)

101. Ivatt no. 46422 is seen shunting on the quay alongside the canal basin on 2nd March 1962. (Ron Herbert)

102. On the same day Ivatt no. 46422 is seen heading towards Lancaster along the canal basin branch at the dock. In the background are wagons stabled on the quay branch. (Ron Herbert)

➔ *Inset: Platforms 1 and 2 at Lancaster were used by passenger services to Glasson Dock as well as services to Barrow, Morecambe and Leeds.*
(Lens of Sutton Association')

103. BR Fairburn class 4 2-6-4T no. 42063 is passing through the level crossing at Glasson Dock light engine on 10th September 1963. (Derrick Codling)

Steam Specials

104. The Stephenson Locomotive Society/Manchester Locomotive Society Northern Fells Rail Tour on 29th May 1960. Seen here is ex-LMS Fairburn 2-6-4T no. 42136. The other locomotive in attendance on that section of the tour was ex-LMS Stanier 'Lobster' class 5F 2-6-0 no. 42952. (Robert Humm collection)

105. The RCTS Glasson Dock tour from Lancaster Castle station is on its way back to the city on 20th June 1964. The train has just left Glasson Dock station and was photographed from the B5290 road almost opposite what is now Brows Farm caravan site. The bridge under the penultimate brake van is an occupation bridge giving access to the foreshore and the locomotive is about to pass over the girder bridge spanning the River Conder - see picture 97. (Noel Machell)

8. St. George's Quay Branch

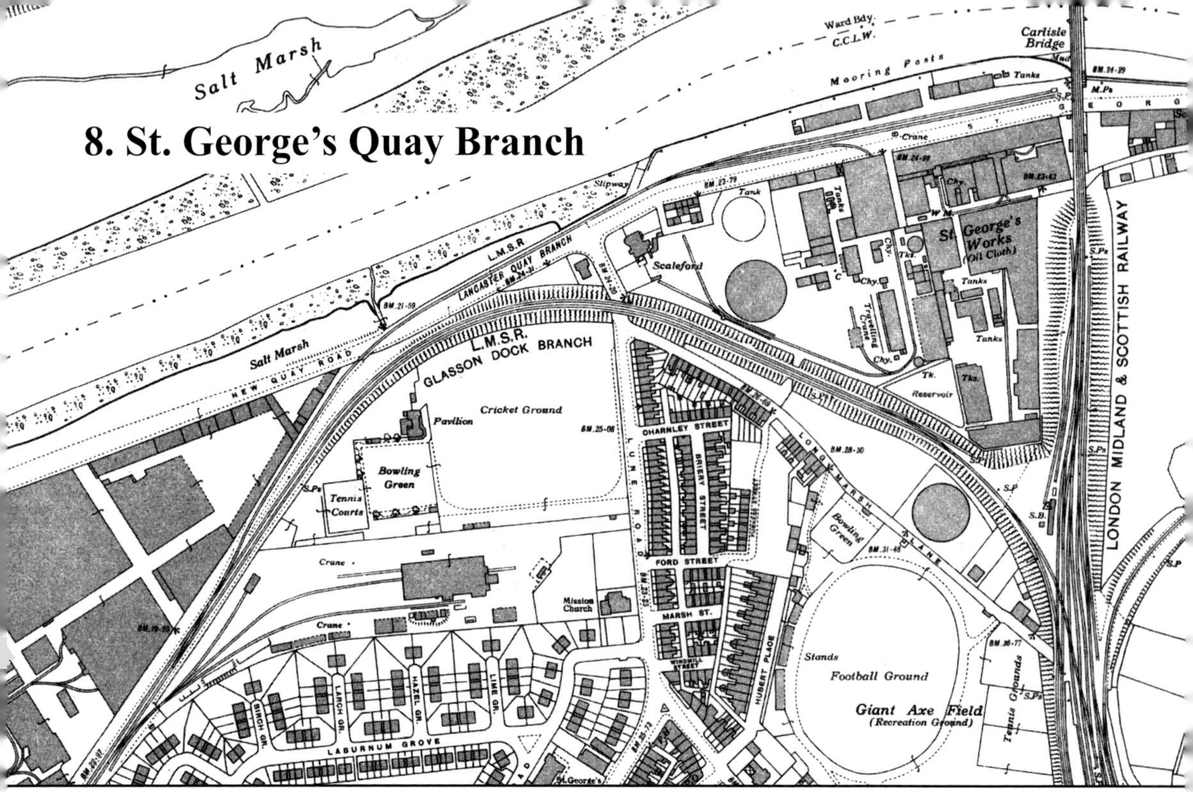

XXXII. This 1939 map shows the extensive industrial activity in that small corner of the city that is all now lost to housing and student accommodation, bar the sports fields. Trains entering St George's Quay branch would proceed towards Glasson and reverse into the quay sidings at Freeman's Wood. Both Williamson's and the Gas Works had internal standard gauge systems.

XXXIII. This is another part of the Carnforth section controllers train board at Preston station. It shows in graphic detail the abundance of sidings serving the NW Gas Board, the LNWR yard and sidings and the extensive Williamson's factory complexes. The J. Williamson & Son Ltd business was founded by James Williamson senior and his son James, who later became Lord Ashton, and took over the Lino and Oil Cloth business. Manufacturing ceased in 1999 and factory buildings were left empty and vandalised until being demolished for housing.

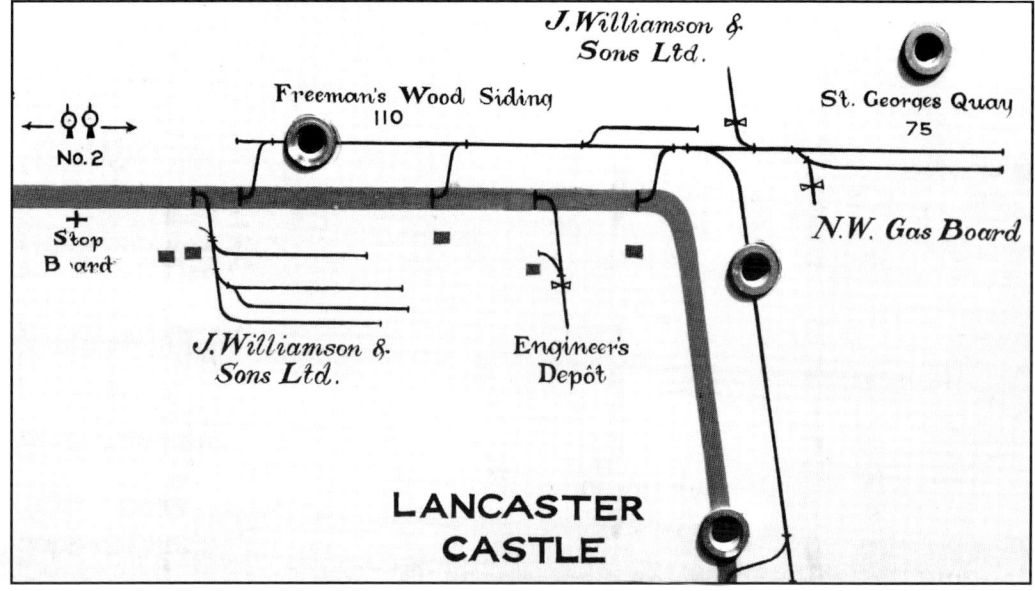

106. This shot taken in July 1966 is a trip working probably of empty vans from Lancaster Castle yard down to the sidings at the Nairn-Williamson Lune Mills floor coverings factory. The locomotive is an unidentified Black 5 presumably from Carnforth working tender first. (Noel Machell)

107. One of Lancaster's Ivatt 2-6-0s possibly no. 46426 ascends the bank to Lancaster Castle in March 1964 with a Williamson's trip working comprising vans loaded with linoleum and empty coal wagons. (Derrick Codling)

108. In this photograph, taken in 1948, the entrance to the engineer's depot can be seen on the right and the extensive Lune Mills complex and siding to the left. Ahead is the line to the quay. The building in the engineer's depot with the curved roof is where the Inspector's Saloon was stabled. From 1890 there was a narrow gauge system in the factory that was extended over the years but by 1935 was disused. (Cumbria Railways Association/Rev. Jackson coll.)

109. On 11th March 1964 Ivatt no. 46422 is seen shunting wagons in the engineer's depot while coupled to condemned Fowler no. 42301 as seen in caption 100. Later the train would proceed to Glasson Dock with a mixed freight and the 2-6-4T destined to become scrap. That same curved roof can be seen behind the second locomotive. (Ron Herbert)

110. Fairburn 2-6-4T no. 42063 is seen shunting at Nairn-Williamson Ltd on 10th September 1963. On the left, wagons can be seen on the incline up to Lancaster Castle station. (Derrick Codling)

111. The Fairburn no. 42063 is seen shunting on Lancaster Quay on 17th September 1963. The photographer recollects that there was only one coal merchant taking deliveries of coal on the quay after Lancaster Gas works closed following the opening of the new joint Lancaster & Morecambe town gas works, which was located on the Midland line between Scale Hall Station & Torrisholme No. 1 Signal Box. In the background across the River Lune a rebuilt ex-LNWR class AM1 three-car EMU is on its way to Morecambe Promenade from Lancaster Castle via Green Ayre and is just about to pull into Scale Hall Station. (Derrick Codling)

112. The rails on the quay were used during the reconstruction of the upper part of Carlisle Bridge carrying the WCML over the River Lune. Seen in this photo on 19th August 1962 are new beams for the rebuild on bogie flats. The original river crossing, known officially as the Lune Viaduct, Bridge No. 2, Lancaster was completed in 1847 with a length of 360ft (110m) and rebuilt by the LNWR in 1866. A survey in the early 1960s indicated that further works were required and the bridge was rebuilt during late 1962-early 1963. The girders were lifted to the required height by use of the cradle built across the tracks on the quay, as seen in the photograph, and moved into position, as required. The original stone piers supporting the bridge are those of the original Lancaster & Carlisle Railway 1847 construction. Throughout the 1960s rebuild, trains continued to use the crossing and from January 1963 on a limited basis, when the two running lines were interlaced, meant only one train was permitted to use the bridge at any one time. Movements were controlled by Lancaster No 4 and Morecambe South Junction boxes in conjunction with the control office at Preston. With use of the bridge restricted as many freight trains as possible were diverted off this section of the WCML on to all possible alternative routes in the northwest. There is a walkway for public use attached to the east side of the bridge. Finally note one of the former Williamson factories behind the wagons; this was demolished in 2022 to make way for student and residential accommodation. (Ron Herbert)

113. Carnforth based ex-LMS Fowler class 3F 0-6-0T 'Jinty' no. 47662 heads an early evening trip working up the 1:50 incline in June 1964 from the Lune Mills sidings bound for Lancaster Castle yards. (Noel Machell)

9. Lancaster Power Station Branch

XXXIV. In this 1968 6ins to 1 mile map the line from Lancaster Castle station runs to the power station on the south side of the canal and the sidings and coal storage on the north side. The former Midland mainline (dotted line on the diagram below) closed on 4th June 1967 and the single-track spur from Lancaster Castle to the power station on 16th March 1976.

Inset: With the cessation of the Morecambe electric services in December 1965, the Overhead Line Equipment on the spur from Lancaster Castle to Green Ayre was removed by 28th June 1966. With the last train from Heysham to the West Riding of Yorkshire running on 3rd June 1967, the former Midland main line tracks, depicted on this map by the dotted line, were later lifted and replaced by a single line connecting with the spur from Lancaster Castle that ran through the centre of the road to the power station complex on Caton Road. Note that the complex is dissected by the Lancaster canal running north-south. With closure of the power station on 26th October 1976, the fireless locomotives were transferred to Heysham nuclear power station in 1977. The facility was later demolished and the site is now occupied by commercial and industrial units off Caton Road, although an electrical substation remains to feed power from the national grid into the Lancaster distribution network. (Diagram: source unknown)

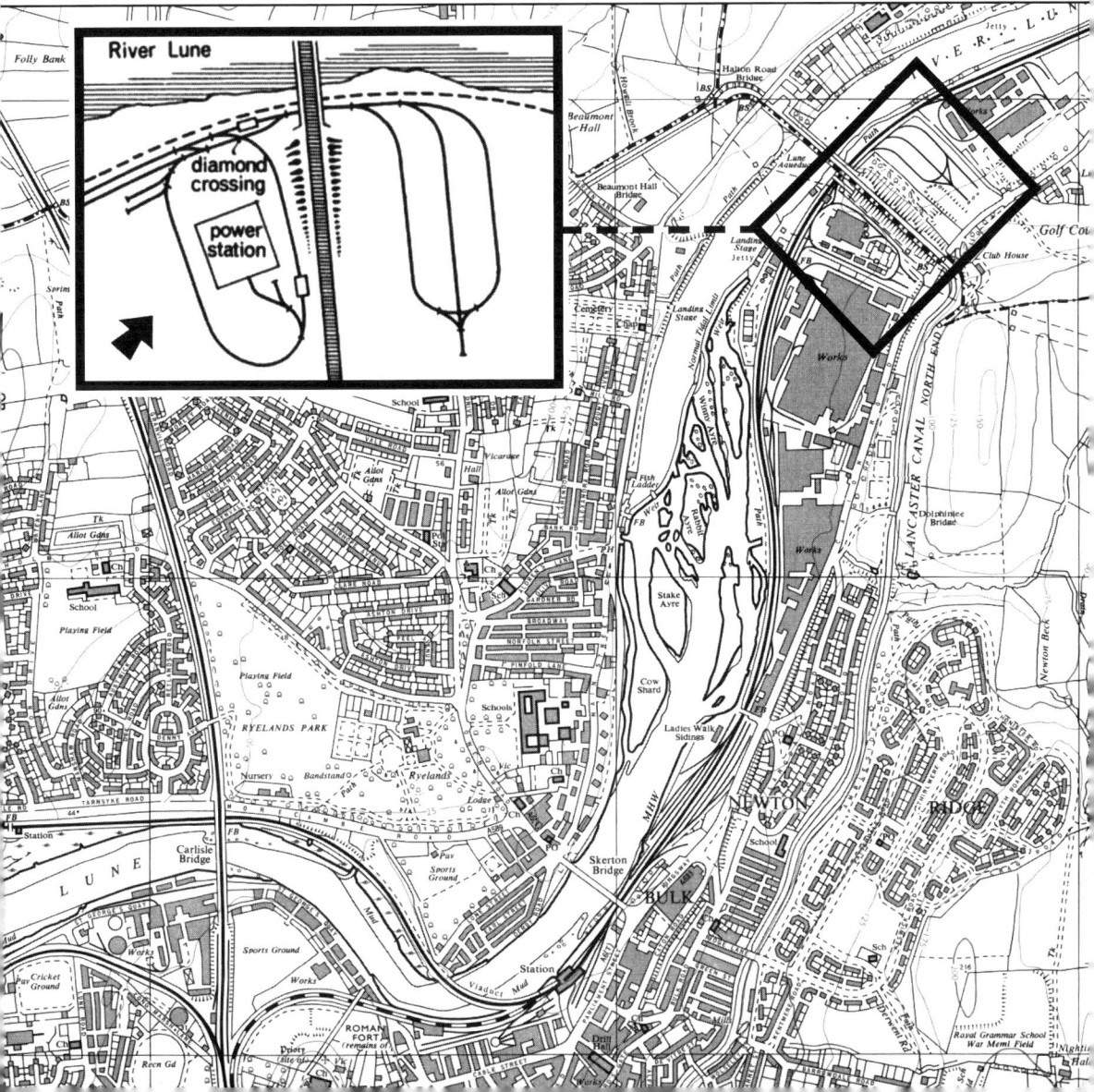

114. An unidentified class 25 is seen heading down the spur towards the site of Lancaster Green Ayre station with loaded coal wagons for the power station some time in either 1974 or 1975.
(Jonathan Dixon)

115. A view of the branch on 10th July 1972 from more or less the same position as in the previous picture. Note that the OLE has been removed and road traffic is using the Greyhound Bridge. A deserted Green Ayre MPD can be seen in the distance; the site of which, along with the former goods shed, is now occupied by a supermarket.
(Keith Holt/KDH Archive)

116. In this circa 1970 shot, the north side of Lancaster Green Ayre station is all but demolished. In the background crossing the River Lune is Skerton Bridge and in the foreground is the relatively new track leading to the power station, which replaced the former Midland metals. (Martin Cruickshank)

117. On 30th March 1976 an unidentified class 25 hauling flatbed wagons is seen crossing the northbound A6/A589 carriageway on the Greyhound Bridge heading towards the site of the former Lancaster Green Ayre station; the train was most likely involved in track-lifting duties at that time, although a section of the track remained in situ on the carriageway for some time pending resurfacing of the road. (Peter Whatley)

118. Looking down from Skerton Bridge at what remained of Lancaster Green Ayre station on 27th April 1973. The station buildings had been demolished by then along with the tracks, save for the new single line to the power station. The site of the former station is now a small public park that is home to a crane from nearby Hornby station goods shed. (Keith Holt/KDH Archive)

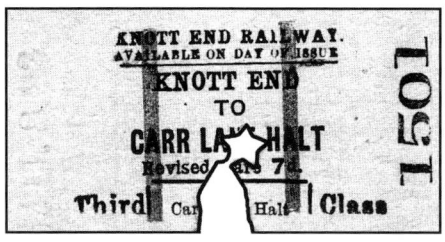

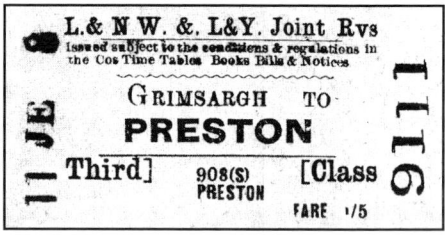

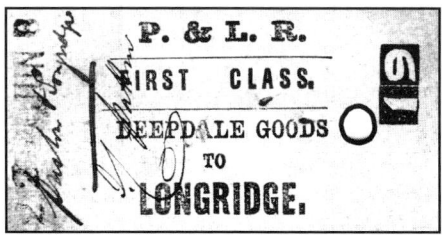

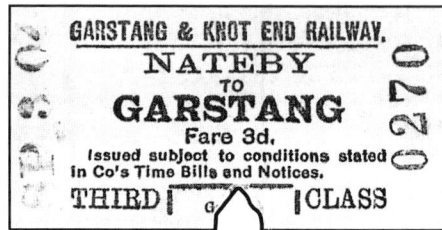

119. Andrew Barclay fireless loco 1572/1917 0-6-0F *No. 1 Lancaster* on shed inside the power station on 9th June 1973. (Les Tindall/Andrew Naylor coll.)

120. In April 1976, class 25 no. 25200 is hauling a track lifting train on the final stages of the incline up to Lancaster station thus marking the removal of the last vestige of the former Midland Line in the city. Ahead is the gasometer at the former Lancaster gas works on St George's Quay. (Jonathan Dixon)

EVOLVING THE
Vic Mitchell and Keith Smith
ULTIMATE RAIL ENCYCLOPEDIA
INTERNATIONAL

126a Camelsdale Road, GU27 3RJ. Tel:01730 813169

A-978 0 906520 B- 978 1 873793 C- 978 1 901706 D-978 1 904474
E - 978 1 906008 F - 978 1 908174 G - 978 1 910356

Our RAILWAY titles are listed below. Please check availability by looking at our website **www.middletonpress.co.uk,** telephoning us or by requesting a Brochure which includes our LATEST RAILWAY TITLES also our TRAMWAY, TROLLEYBUS, MILITARY and COASTAL series.

email:info@middletonpress.co.uk

A
Abergavenny to Merthyr C 91 8
Abertillery & Ebbw Vale Lines D 84 5
Aberystwyth to Carmarthen E 90 1
Alnmouth to Berwick G 50 0
Alton - Branch Lines to A 11 6
Ambergate to Buxton G 28 9
Ambergate to Mansfield G 39 5
Andover to Southampton A 82 6
Ascot - Branch Lines around A 64 2
Ashburton - Branch Line to B 95 4
Ashford - Steam to Eurostar B 67 1
Ashford to Dover A 48 2
Austrian Narrow Gauge D 04 3
Avonmouth - BL around D 42 5
Aylesbury to Rugby D 91 3
B
Baker Street to Uxbridge D 90 6
Bala to Llandudno E 87 1
Banbury to Birmingham D 27 2
Banbury to Cheltenham E 63 5
Bangor to Holyhead F 01 7
Bangor to Portmadoc E 72 7
Barking to Southend C 80 2
Barmouth to Pwllheli E 53 6
Barry - Branch Lines around D 50 0
Bartlow - Branch Lines to F 27 7
Basingstoke to Salisbury A 89 4
Bath Green Park to Bristol C 36 9
Bath to Evercreech Junction A 60 4
Beamish 40 years on rails E94 9
Beattock to Carstairs G 84 5
Bedford to Wellingborough D 31 9
Berwick to Drem F 64 2
Berwick to St. Boswells F 75 8
B'ham to Tamworth & Nuneaton F 63 5
Birkenhead to West Kirby F 61 1
Birmingham to Wolverhampton E253
Blackburn to Hellifield F 95 6
Blackburn to Skipton G 85 2
Bletchley to Cambridge D 94 4
Bletchley to Rugby E 07 9
Bodmin - Branch Lines around B 83 1
Bolton to Preston G 61 6
Boston to Lincoln F 80 2
Bournemouth to Evercreech Jn A 46 8
Bradshaw's History F18 5
Bradshaw's Rail Times 1850 F 13 0
Branch Lines series - see town names
Brecon to Neath D 43 2
Brecon to Newport D 16 6
Brecon to Newtown E 06 2
Brighton to Eastbourne A 16 1
Brighton to Worthing A 03 1
Bristol to Taunton D 03 6
Bromley South to Rochester B 23 7
Bromsgrove to Birmingham D 87 6
Bromsgrove to Gloucester D 73 9
Broxbourne to Cambridge F16 1
Brunel - A railtour D 74 6
Bude - Branch Line to B 29 9
Burnham to Evercreech Jn B 68 0
Buxton to Stockport G 32 6
C
Cambridge to Ely D 55 5
Canterbury - BLs around B 58 9
Cardiff to Dowlais (Cae Harris) E 47 5
Cardiff to Pontypridd E 95 6
Cardiff to Swansea E 42 0
Carlisle to Beattock G 69 2
Carlisle to Hawick E 85 7
Carmarthen to Fishguard E 66 6
Caterham & Tattenham Corner B251
Central & Southern Spain NG E 91 8
Chard and Yeovil - BLs a C 30 7
Charing Cross to Orpington A 96 3
Cheddar - Branch Line to B 90 9
Cheltenham to Andover C 43 7
Cheltenham to Redditch D 81 4
Chesterfield to Lincoln G 21 0
Chester to Birkenhead F 21 5
Chester to Manchester F 51 2
Chester to Rhyl E 93 2
Chester to Warrington F 40 6
Chichester to Portsmouth A 14 7
Clacton and Walton - BLs to F 04 8
Clapham Jn to Beckenham Jn B 36 7
Cleobury Mortimer - BLs a E 18 5
Clevedon & Portishead - BLs to D180
Consett to South Shields E 57 4
Cornwall Narrow Gauge D 56 2
Corris and Vale of Rheidol E 65 9
Coventry to Leicester G 00 5
Craven Arms to Llandeilo E 35 2
Craven Arms to Wellington E 33 8
Crawley to Littlehampton A 34 5
Crewe to Manchester F 57 4
Crewe to Wigan G 12 8
Cromer - Branch Lines around C 26 0
Cromford and High Peak G 35 7
Croydon to East Grinstead B 48 0
Crystal Palace & Catford Loop B 87 1
Cyprus Narrow Gauge E 13 0
D
Darjeeling Revisited F 09 3
Darlington Leamside Newcastle E 28 4
Darlington to Newcastle D 98 2
Dartford to Sittingbourne B 34 3
Denbigh - Branch Lines around F 32 1
Derby to Chesterfield G 11 1
Derby to Nottingham G 45 6
Derby to Stoke-on-Trent F 93 2
Derwent Valley - BL to the D 06 7
Devon Narrow Gauge E 09 3
Didcot to Banbury D 02 9
Didcot to Swindon C 84 0
Didcot to Winchester C 13 0
Diss to Norwich G 22 7
Dorset & Somerset NG D 76 0
Douglas - Laxey - Ramsey E 75 8
Douglas to Peel C 88 8
Douglas to Port Erin C 55 0
Douglas to Ramsey D 39 5
Dover to Ramsgate A 78 9
Drem to Edinburgh G 06 7
Dublin Northwards in 1950s E 31 4
Dunstable - Branch Lines to E 27 7
E
Ealing to Slough C 42 0
Eastbourne to Hastings A 27 7
East Croydon to Three Bridges A 53 6
Eastern Spain Narrow Gauge E 56 7
East Grinstead - BLs to A 07 9
East Kent Light Railway A 61 1
East London - Branch Lines of C 44 4
East London Line B 80 0
East of Norwich - Branch Lines E 69 7
Effingham Junction - BLs a A 74 1
Ely to Norwich C 90 1
Enfield Town & Palace Gates D 32 6
Epsom to Horsham A 30 7
Eritrean Narrow Gauge E 38 3
Euston to Harrow & Wealdstone C 89 5
Exeter to Barnstaple B 15 2
Exeter to Newton Abbot C 49 9
Exeter to Tavistock B 69 5
Exmouth - Branch Lines to B 00 8
F
Fairford - Branch Line to A 52 9
Falmouth, Helston & St. Ives C 74 1
Fareham to Salisbury A 67 3
Faversham to Dover B 05 3
Felixstowe & Aldeburgh - BL to D 20 3
Fenchurch Street to Barking C 20 8
Festiniog - 50 yrs of enterprise C 83 3
Festiniog 1946-55 E 01 7
Festiniog in the Fifties B 68 8
Festiniog in the Sixties B 91 6
Ffestiniog in Colour 1955-82 F 25 3
Finsbury Park to Alexandra Pal C 02 8
French Metre Gauge Survivors F 88 8
Frome to Bristol B 77 0
G
Gainsborough to Sheffield G 17 3
Galashiels to Edinburgh F 52 9
Gloucester to Bristol D 35 7
Gloucester to Cardiff D 66 1
Gosport - Branch Lines around A 36 9
Greece Narrow Gauge D 72 2
Guildford to Redhill A 63 5
H
Hampshire Narrow Gauge D 36 4
Harrow to Watford D 14 2
Harwich & Hadleigh - BLs to F 02 4
Harz Revisited F 62 8
Hastings to Ashford A 37 6
Hawick to Galashiels F 36 9
Hawkhurst - Branch Line to A 66 6
Hayling - Branch Line to A 12 3
Hay-on-Wye - BL around D 92 0
Haywards Heath to Seaford A 28 4
Hemel Hempstead - BLs to D 88 3
Henley, Windsor & Marlow - BLa C77 2
Hereford to Newport D 54 8
Hertford & Hatfield - BLs a E 58 1
Hertford Loop E 71 0
Hexham to Carlisle D 75 3
Hexham to Hawick F 08 6
Hitchin to Peterborough D 07 4
Horsham - Branch Lines to A 02 4
Hull, Hornsea and Withernsea G 27 2
Hull to Scarborough G 60 9
Huntingdon - Branch Line to A 93 2
I
Ilford to Shenfield C 97 0
Ilfracombe - Branch Line to B 21 3
Ilkeston to Chesterfield G 26 5
Inverkeithing to Thornton Jct G 76 0
Ipswich to Diss F 81 9
Ipswich to Saxmundham C 41 3
Isle of Man Railway Journey F 94 9
Isle of Wight Lines - 50 yrs C 12 3
Italy Narrow Gauge F 17 8
K
Kent Narrow Gauge C 45 1
Kettering to Nottingham F 82-6
Kidderminster to Shrewsbury E 10 9
Kingsbridge - Branch Line to C 98 7
Kings Cross to Potters Bar E 62 8
King's Lynn to Hunstanton F 58 1
Kingston & Hounslow Loops A 83 3
Kingswear - Branch Line to C 17 8
L
Lambourn - Branch Line to C 70 3
Lancaster to Oxenholme G 77 7
Launceston & Princetown - BLs C 19 2
Leeds to Selby G 47 0
Leek - Branch Line From G 01 2
Leicester to Burton F 85 7
Leicester to Nottingham G 15 9
Lewisham to Dartford A 92 5
Lincoln to Cleethorpes F 56 7
Lincoln to Doncaster G 03 6
Lines around Newmarket G 54 8
Lines around Stamford F 98 7
Lines around Wimbledon B 75 6
Lines North of Stoke G 29 6
Liverpool to Runcorn G 72 2
Liverpool Street to Chingford D 01 2
Liverpool Street to Ilford C 34 5
Llandeilo to Swansea E 46 8
London Bridge to Addiscombe B 20 6
London Bridge to East Croydon A 58 1
Longmoor - Branch Lines to A 41 3
Looe - Branch Line to C 22 2
Loughborough to Ilkeston G 24 1
Loughborough to Nottingham F 68 0
Lowestoft - BLs around E 40 6
Ludlow to Hereford E 14 7
Lydney - Branch Lines around E 26 0
Lyme Regis - Branch Line to A 45 1
Lynton - Branch Line to B 04 6
M
Machynlleth to Barmouth E 54 3
Maesteg and Tondu Lines F 06 2
Majorca & Corsica Narrow Gauge F 41 3
Manchester to Bacup G 46 3
Mansfield to Doncaster G 23 4
March - Branch Lines around B 09 1
Market Drayton - BLs around F 67 3
Market Harborough to Newark F 86 4
Marylebone to Rickmansworth D 49 4
Melton Constable to Yarmouth Bch E031
Midhurst - Branch Lines of E 78 9
Midhurst - Branch Lines to F 00 0
Minehead - Branch Line to A 80 2
Monmouth - Branch Lines to E 20 8
Monmouthshire Eastern Valleys D 71 5
Moretonhampstead - BL to C 27 7
Moreton-in-Marsh to Worcester D 26 5
Morpeth to Bellingham F 87 1
Mountain Ash to Neath D 80 7
N
Newark to Doncaster F 78 9
Newbury to Westbury C 66 6
Newcastle to Alnmouth G 36 4
Newcastle to Hexham D 69 2
Newmarket to Haughley & Laxfield G 71 5
New Mills to Sheffield G 44 9
Newport (IOW) - Branch Lines to A 26 0
Newquay - Branch Lines to C 71 0
Newton Abbot to Plymouth C 60 4
Newtown to Aberystwyth E 41 3
Northampton to Peterborough F 92 5
North East German NG D 44 9
Northern Alpine Narrow Gauge F 37 6
Northern Spain Narrow Gauge E 83 3
North London Line B 94 7
North of Birmingham F 55 0
North of Grimsby - Branch Lines G 09 8
North Woolwich - BLs around C 65 9
Nottingham to Boston F 70 3
Nottingham to Kirkby Bentinck G 38 8
Nottingham to Lincoln F 43 7
Nottingham to Mansfield G 52 4
Nuneaton to Loughborough G 08 1
O
Ongar - Branch Line to E 05 5
Orpington to Tonbridge B 03 9
Oswestry - Branch Lines around E 60 4
Oswestry to Whitchurch E 81 9
Oxford to Bletchley D 57 9
Oxford to Moreton-in-Marsh D 15 9
P
Paddington to Ealing C 37 6
Paddington to Princes Risborough C819
Padstow - Branch Line to B 54 1
Peebles Loop G 19 7
Pembroke and Cardigan - BLs to F 29 1
Peterborough to Kings Lynn E 32 1
Peterborough to Lincoln F 89 5
Peterborough to Newark F 72 7
Plymouth - BLs around B 98 5
Plymouth to St. Austell C 63 5
Pontypool to Mountain Ash D 65 4
Pontypridd to Merthyr F 14 7
Pontypridd to Port Talbot E 86 4
Porthmadog 1954-94 - BLa B 31 2
Portmadoc 1923-46 - BLa B 13 8
Portsmouth to Southampton A 31 4
Portugal Narrow Gauge E 67 3
Potters Bar to Cambridge D 70 8
Preston & Lancaster - BLs around G 82 1
Preston to Blackpool G 16 6
Preston to the Fylde Coast G 81 4
Preston to Lancaster G 74 6
Princes Risborough - BL to D 05 0
Princes Risborough to Banbury C 85 7
R
Railways to Victory C 16 1
Reading to Basingstoke B 27 5
Reading to Didcot C 79 6
Reading to Guildford A 47 5
Redhill to Ashford A 73 4
Return to Blaenau 1970-82 C 64 2
Rhyl to Bangor F 15 4
Rhymney & New Tredegar Lines E 48 2
Rickmansworth to Aylesbury D 61 6
Romania & Bulgaria NG E 23 9
Ross-on-Wye - BLs around E 30 7
Ruabon to Barmouth E 84 0
Rugby to Birmingham E 37 6
Rugby to Loughborough F 12 3
Rugby to Stafford F 07 9
Rugeley to Stoke-on-Trent F 90 1
Ryde to Ventnor A 19 2
S
Salisbury to Westbury B 39 8
Salisbury to Yeovil B 06 0
Sardinia and Sicily Narrow Gauge F 50 5
Saxmundham to Yarmouth C 69 7
Saxony & Baltic Germany Revisited F 71 0
Saxony Narrow Gauge D 47 0
Scunthorpe to Doncaster G 34 0
Seaton & Sidmouth - BLs to A 95 6
Selsey - Branch Line to A 04 8
Sheerness - Branch Line to B 16 2
Sheffield towards Manchester G 18 0
Shenfield to Ipswich E 96 3
Shildon to Stockton G 79 1
Shrewsbury - Branch Line to A 86 4
Shrewsbury to Chester E 70 3
Shrewsbury to Crewe F 48 2
Shrewsbury to Ludlow E 21 5
Shrewsbury to Newtown E 29 1
Sirhowy Valley Line E 12 3
Sittingbourne to Ramsgate A 90 1
Skegness & Mablethorpe - BL to F 84 0
Slough to Newbury C 56 7
South African Two-foot gauge E 51 2
Southampton to Bournemouth A 42 0
Southend & Southminster BLs E 76 5
Southern Alpine Narrow Gauge F 22 2
South London Line B 46 6
South Lynn to Norwich City F 03 1
Southwold - Branch Line to A 15 4
Spalding - Branch Lines around E 52 9
Spalding to Grimsby F 65 9 6
Stafford to Chester F 34 5
Stafford to Wellington F 59 8
St Albans to Bedford D 08 1
St. Austell to Penzance C 67 3
St. Boswell to Berwick F 44 4
Stourbridge to Wolverhampton E 16 1
St. Pancras to Barking D 68 5
St. Pancras to Folkestone E 88 8
St. Pancras to St. Albans C 78 9
Stratford to Cheshunt F 53 6
Stratford-u-Avon to Birmingham D 77 7
Stratford-u-Avon to Cheltenham C 25 3
Sudbury - Branch Lines to F 19 2
Surrey Narrow Gauge C 87 1
Sussex Narrow Gauge C 68 0
Swaffham - Branch Lines around F 97 0
Swanage to 1999 - BL to A 33 8
Swanley to Ashford B 45 9
Swansea - Branch Lines around F 38 3
Swansea to Carmarthen E 59 8
Swindon to Bristol C 96 3
Swindon to Gloucester D 46 3
Swindon to Newport D 30 2
Swiss Narrow Gauge C 94 9
T
Talyllyn 60 E 98 7
Tamworth to Derby F 76 5
Taunton to Barnstaple B 60 2
Taunton to Exeter C 82 6
Taunton to Minehead F 39 0
Tavistock to Plymouth B 88 6
Tenterden - Branch Line to A 21 5
Three Bridges to Brighton A 35 2
Tilbury Loop C 86 4
Tiverton - BLs around C 62 8
Tivetshall to Beccles D 41 8
Tonbridge to Hastings A 44 4
Torrington - Branch Lines to B 37 4
Tourist Railways of France G 04 3
Towcester - BLs around E 39 0
Tunbridge Wells BLs A 32 1
U
Upwell - Branch Line to B 64 0
Uttoxeter to Macclesfield G 05 0
Uttoxetor to Buxton G 33 3
V
Victoria to Bromley South A 98 7
Victoria to East Croydon A 40 6
Vivarais Revisited E 08 6
W
Walsall Routes F 45 1
Wantage - Branch Line to D 25 8
Wareham to Swanage 50 yrs D 09 8
Watercress Line G 75 3
Waterloo to Windsor A 54 3
Waterloo to Woking A 38 3
Watford to Leighton Buzzard D 45 6
Wellingborough to Leicester F 73 4
Welshpool to Llanfair E 49 9
Wenford Bridge to Fowey C 09 3
Wennington to Morecambe G 58 6
Westbury to Bath B 55 8
Westbury to Taunton C 76 5
West Cornwall Mineral Rlys D 48 7
West Croydon to Epsom B 08 4
West German Narrow Gauge D 93 7
West London - BLs of C 50 5
West London Line B 84 8
West Somerset Railway G 78 4
West Wiltshire - BLs of D 12 8
Weymouth - BLs A 65 9
Willesden Jn to Richmond B 71 8
Wimbledon to Beckenham C 58 1
Wimbledon to Epsom B 62 6
Wimborne - BLs around A 97 0
Wirksworth - Branch Lines to G 10 4
Wisbech - BLs around C 01 7
Witham & Kelvedon - BLs a E 82 6
Woking to Alton A 59 8
Woking to Portsmouth A 25 3
Woking to Southampton A 55 0
Wolverhampton to Shrewsbury E 44 4
Wolverhampton to Stafford F 79 6
Worcester to Birmingham D 97 5
Worcester to Hereford D 38 8
Worthing to Chichester A 06 2
Wrexham to New Brighton F 47 5
Wroxham - BLs around F 31 4
Y
Yeovil - 50 yrs change C 38 3
Yeovil to Dorchester A 76 5
Yeovil to Exeter A 91 8
York to Scarborough F 23 9